DEAR FUTURE H

Lyrics and exegesis of Rou Reynolds for
the music of Enter Shikari 2006–2019

FABER *ff* MUSIC

For their support, guidance and patience I'd like to thank my Mum, Dad & Brother. Chris, Rob & Rory. Ian Johnsen. Lucy and everyone at Faber Music. Mike and everyone at Universal Publishing. Katherine Melling. Peter and everyone at PIAS. Everyone who has released or bought our music around the world.

Lyrics by Rou Reynolds
Music by Enter Shikari
© Universal Music Publishing Ltd.
All Rights Reserved.

Creative Direction from Something-Somewhere
Original layout design by Jon Eley

© 2019 by Faber Music Ltd.
This edition first published by Faber Music Ltd. in 2019
Dear Future Historians first published by Faber Music Ltd. in 2017
The Spark first published by Faber Music Ltd. in 2018
Bloomsbury House
74–77 Great Russell Street
London WC1B 3DA

Printed and bound in Turkey by Imago
All Rights Reserved

ISBN: 0-571-54112-7
EAN: 978-0-571-54112-6

To buy Faber Music publications or to find out about the full range of titles available, please contact your local music retailer or Faber Music sales enquiries:

Faber Music Limited, Burnt Mill, Elizabeth Way, Harlow CM20 2HX
Tel: +44 (0)1279 82 89 82   Fax: +44 (0)1279 82 89 83
sales@fabermusic.com   fabermusicstore.com

Tom Pullen, 2019

CONTENTS

08 TAKE TO THE
SKIES ERA

Take To The Skies
Mothership
Anything Can Happen In The
  Next Half Hour
Labyrinth
No Sssweat
Today Won't Go Down In
  History
Return To Energiser
Sorry, You're Not A Winner
Johnny Sniper
Adieu
Ok, Time For Plan B
The Feast
Kicking Back On The Surface
  Of Your Cheek
Acid Nation
Keep It On Ice
We Can Breathe In Space, They
  Just Don't Want Us To Escape

58 COMMON
DREADS ERA

Common Dreads
Solidarity
Step Up
Juggernauts
Wall
Zzzonked
Havoc A
No Sleep Tonight
Gap In The Fence
Havoc B
Antwerpen
The Jester
Hectic
Fanfare For The Conscious Man
All Eyes On The Saint
Tribalism
Thumper

104 A FLASH FLOOD OF
COLOUR ERA

Destabilise
Quelle Surprise
System...
...Meltdown
Sssnakepit
Search Party
Arguing With Thermometers
Stalemate
Gandhi Mate, Gandhi
Warm Smiles Do Not Make
   You Welcome Here
Pack Of Thieves
Hello Tyrannosaurus, Meet
   Tyrannicide
Constellations
The Paddington Frisk
Rat Race
Radiate

154 THE
MINDSWEEP ERA

The Appeal & The Mindsweep I
The One True Colour
Anaesthetist
The Last Garrison
Never Let Go Of The Microscope
Myopia
Torn Apart
The Bank Of England
There's A Price On Your Head
Dear Future Historians
The Appeal & The Mindsweep II
Slipshod
Redshift
Hoodwinker

210 THE
SPARK ERA

The Sights
Live Outside
Take My Country Back
Airfield
Rabble Rouser
Shinrin-Yoku
Undercover Agents
The Revolt Of The Atoms
An Ode To Lost Jigsaw Pieces
Stop The Clocks

London, UK. Dec 2015 – Corinne Cumming

Darlings,

In this book you will find the lyrics to every single Enter Shikari song officially released thus far.

Accompanying these you will find explanatory essays that document my various inspirations and intentions.

Please excuse me if I've been too verbose or banged on about something for far too long here and there, the thought of being a published author may have gone to my head. I do try and go into great detail though, sometimes deconstructing individual lines one by one. I have really pulled back the curtain, this is for those of you who like to immerse yourselves in art and ponder its construction and intentions. I'm certain that this is something I would've lapped up from my favourite bands growing up, so I'm hoping some of you out there will get similar satisfaction.

You can read this book from front to back or treat it like a reference book if you like (i.e. when you're listening to Shikari, pick up the book and use the index at the back to find the song and have a gander at the accompanying essay). I would recommend listening to each song either before, after, or during reading its essay though, just so you can feel, as well as read, what my intentions were.

It struck me whilst collating all of this, just what a back catalogue of music we have now, and just how incredible it is that a band like ours - Independent. Niche. Progressive. - has had the opportunity to be around for such a solid amount of time. Of course not a solid amount of time like the amount of time the quaint folklores that inspire 'Antwerpen' or 'All Eyes On The Saint' have been around, nor a solid amount of time like the amount of time since hanging was a regular occurrence in London Town (the focus of 'The Paddington Frisk'), or the amount of time capitalism has been around (the focus of 'The Bank Of England') and *certainly* not a solid amount of time in comparison to the dizzyingly vast two trillion years in the future, which is the temporal setting for 'Redshift'. But still, I'm grateful for the amount of time I've been able to spend creating and performing music. Waking up and writing music or lyrics is honestly what I live for. I thank you, reader, for your continued support: the fact that we are still going from strength to strength all around the world emboldens us. Big up everyone who has shown us support and thank you for picking up this book. I beckon you to go forth, delve into my head and dawdle about, please excuse the mess.

Rou
x

TAKE
TO TH
SKIES
ERA

Tokyo, Japan. Jan 2007 — Ian Johnsen

Take To The Skies. Album sleeve by Keaton Henson

ENTER SHIKARI

… shit!

"I've been hiding here for a thousand years, waiting for your ghost"
Your life's about to flash before your eyes

Stand your ground; this is ancient land
I was guided here by the spirit's hand
We shall meet, at hell's gate
This is fate

"Not all is lost" the spirits shriek
You will be hunted, we shall seek
Perseverance, turn the page …
Enter Shikari

We're not hiding now
I'm in the zone

And still we will be here standing like statues

Looking back now, I'm quite surprised we chose to open our debut album with a self-titled track. I honestly remember being quite anxious about the whole affair. A self-titled track is guaranteed to have extra stamina and a longer lease of life. People often also expect a self-titled track to be an insight into the artist's outlook or purpose. It's supposed to be an offering that contains the main thrust of their ideas, the essence of what they're about. That's a lot to lay on the table in the very first audio transmission you release as a band. Truly diving in at the deepest of ends.

I think though, with everything said and done, I'm fairly content with this as the opening salvo to our first album. It conveys a simple message amidst a heavy dose of mysticism and metaphor (a style that is so prominent throughout this early Shikari era). It also contains the line "And still we will be here, standing like statues"; which has become an enduring statement, an eternal chant that we still hear shouted from the audience at almost every show.

The song is an anxious pre-battle conversation between two people. It introduces the main themes of the album (and subsequently themes that are central to Shikari's whole catalogue): Perspective, Unity and Perseverance. I play with and exploit the use of a timeline throughout the track, introducing a feeling almost of disorientation. "I've been hiding here for a thousand years" and "ancient" establish a sense of the past, whereas the future is invoked with lines like "you will be hunted" and "and still we will be here". Even just the word 'fate' itself is entangled with temporal depth; implying something that is meant to happen.

With the word 'ancient' I hoped to evoke images of a time when life was very different. I hoped to elicit visions of past civilisations with different values, behaviours and traditions, in order to highlight the fact that many of the things we believe now will also end up confined to the history books.

I was attempting to create an awareness of the present. What's done is done, we can only now plan for the future. Even "Your life's about to flash before your eyes" is a statement of what is to come. Death could always be around the corner but, until you meet him, you can still change a great deal of that inevitable deathbed montage.

Many of the bands we knew of at this time – whether local contemporaries or bigger acts – were talking about their personal lives, about self-betterment and emotional strength (or the lack of). I wanted to speak about the progress not just of my own behaviour as one human being, but that of our whole species. I think the influence of overtly political hardcore punk scenes helped provoke this grandiose desire, but also it felt like this postmodern, almost extravagant style of music we had created suited the bigger, grander themes so well.

The music of *Take To The Skies* – love it or hate it – was inclusive, multifaceted and extensive in its influences and textures. This encouraged me to go beyond the personal. I wanted to make music with which to address our species. The cockiness, the almost self-aggrandisement here is interesting to look back on. I mean, who was I to address our species? But I think that's why the track is written in such a cryptic manner. It didn't come from the position of a lofty, overconfident, First Year at university, Politics major. I can tell you it was done sheepishly. I was always an "I've got so much to say but I don't even like putting my hand up in class to answer a question 'cos everyone will look at me" type kid.

Fear of being publicly embarrassed, proven wrong, thought of as immature, silly or naive: that has always been a major driving force behind me becoming politically and socially active over the past decade. For all its negatives and hardships, this is perhaps one of the benefits of generalised anxiety disorder. It sneaks ambition in the back-door, purely through fear!

Coming out of secondary school in an era when homophobia and sexism were part of every other schoolboy jibe, where music divided students into warring cliques, and where racism could still be heard in the scuffles outside pubs on a Friday night, I felt it important to start the album by stating that no one should have to hide who they are for fear of being ostracised or bullied. "We're not hiding," the repeated call.

Perspective, Unity, Perseverance.

Cardiff, UK. Feb 2016 – Alexey Makhov

MOTHERSHIP

"Go tell all your friends that this is the end
This is the end"

I don't understand a word you're saying
What are the clouds running from?
There's something in the air tonight
Something is wrong, spit it out!

"I just fell from the Mothership
They said that *'your answers were always lying on the ocean bed'*

There's something in the air
Tonight, I'm wide awake
And I'll plead with a thousand voices … I am sane
My soul felt so safe up there
No self-centred natives destroying our earth"

"Walk the plank
Your answers were always lying on the ocean bed"

As with many of the tracks on *Take To The Skies*, 'Mothership' had already been a staple song in our live set for a while. An earlier version was released as a single in 2006, accompanied by our first music video. You can now only hear that recording on the early B-sides and rarities mini-album *The Zone*. I personally prefer the earlier version; there's an endearing rawness and an untidiness to it. The vocal feels much stronger too (one of my big regrets about *Take To The Skies* is rushing the vocal recording whilst I had health problems, resulting in some rather grating, dry and weak shouted vocals across the record).

Perhaps surprisingly, this is our only song about alien abduction. It started off life as somewhat of an in-joke. At the time, a favourite track of ours to blast in the van whilst on tour was Outhere Brothers' 'Boom Boom Boom', which contains the line, "I just fell from the Mothership". I can remember reciting the bars to that tune; playing round with it until eventually it got warped into the belted, almost operatic chorus melody we hear today.

The early ambition to say something with our music, coupled with the desire not to take ourselves too seriously, is probably what gave birth to this wildly fanciful and over-the-top set of lyrics. (To this day I'm frustrated by the supposed requirement of sombreness to make a relevant point. The sedation of humour doesn't make a point any more significant or virtuous. Music, art, comedy, politics, science … they shouldn't be as compartmentalised, uncommunicative and segregated as they often are.)

The lyrics introduce someone who brings a rather gloomy message, having had first contact with extraterrestrials. If you imagine a crazed person running at you yelling out that first line "Go tell all your friends that this is the end", that is the shock, the fear and the bewilderment I wanted to convey with that opening heavy section.

The first verse is the befuddled reply demanding an explanation, which then comes in the chorus. The warning that the abductee received was of the dire predicted effects of anthropogenic climate change. The "answers" that were "lying on the ocean bed" refers to the bleaching of coral reefs, one of the earliest warning signs of global warming that had been widely researched during the late 1990s. Coral reefs are among the most sensitive ecosystems to long-term climate change. Elevated sea surface temperatures can cause coral to lose their symbiotic algae, which is essential for the nutrition and colour of corals. When the algae die, corals appear white and are referred to as bleached.

"There's something in the air" refers to the rise in carbon dioxide, methane and other greenhouse gases that we began to see in the atmosphere towards the middle of the 20th century. The fight that the abductee is forced to endure to prove his sanity after such wild accusations is similar to the frustration that scientists have felt when up against the corporate and political powers that have denied climate science and impeded humanity's progress since this threat was discovered.

"My soul felt so safe up there, no self-centred natives destroying our earth" – I remember wanting my fictitious aliens to be benign. Apart from E.T. (a film that, ironically enough, scared the shit out of me as a kid), almost *all* films involving aliens had the extraterrestrials depicted as mindless and blood thirsty. I wanted my aliens to be a helpful and peaceful, an almost maternal species. I think that's a more logical stance too. One must imagine that for a species to discover and implement intergalactic space travel, they would have had to solve the petty provincial problems of nuclear threats, super-weapons and inter-species warfare; otherwise they wouldn't have survived through those advances in technology. A sane and successful species would attain equal progress in temperance and humanity, as it would in technology.

But, as safe as our abductee felt away with his new friends, he is ultimately made to "walk the plank" and plummet back down to earth, to become a messenger and spread their warning far and wide.

Nottingham, UK. Feb 2016 – Alexey Makhov

ANYTHING CAN HAPPEN IN THE NEXT HALF HOUR

His eyes are locked on her
Her eyes are fixed elsewhere
He's confident but he's not aware …
She doesn't care

Their only connection is the silence that they both grasp
He's lost control but she's not aware …
Of his stare

Everything seems to intimidate him
With the strobe lights flashing, her body's jolting
But cracking as his eyes spilt in two …
If only she knew

The curtain goes down on him again

Everything seems to be closing in on her
It feels just like she is being hunted
But it's alright, it's all good, she's not aware …
Of his stare

We've had this date from the beginning

Who remains when the curtain falls?
Who remains when the curtain goes down?

London, UK. Feb 2016 – Alexey Makhov

LABYRINTH

… help!
The air turns black, the birds drop from the sky
This eagle has landed, I'm choking on your pride
And the walls are closing in
And you don't appreciate that in my hands tonight
Is where your fate lies
Her face drains …

Stand up and take a bow
You have no reason to celebrate
You're lost in the labyrinth, scream now it's not too late

Nothing seems to break the walls down
We'll break the walls down!

(Well it looks like the end is nigh for our friends here
He's finding it hard to keep his head
Especially with his girl screaming in his ear
We've got to ask ourselves do they deserve this?
It's a minute to make you mind up o' clock
Speak now or forever hold your peace!)

Will he make it out?
I hope he makes it out!
He's gonna make it out!
He's got to make it out!

You're lost in the labyrinth

Wrexham, UK. Feb 2016 – Alexey Makhov

NO SSSWEAT

Where's your respect?
Why bite the hand that feeds you?
It's not over yet
Plenty more fingers for you to nibble

I'd like to see you get your teeth round this
I'm sure your jaw will sorely be missed

Not even salt can make your hands taste good
I'm still crunching your lifeline

You do this every fucking time
No sweat, no tears, no guilt

Blood fills your palms
Do this one more time and I'll bite your fucking fingers off

Some of the tracks on *Take To The Skies* are entirely made up of verses of
non sequitur gobbledegook[1] ('Return To Energiser' and 'Sorry, You're Not
A Winner' being the most obvious examples). I recall being a fan of overly
intricate, confusing, narratives at the time. This track, 'No Sssweat', shares that
bombardment of arbitrary imagery and metaphor, but it *does* however have a
basic intention.

I'd always felt slightly frustrated with fashion, growing up. Firstly the sectarian
nature of 'style', the cliques it helped differentiate, the pressure it built on students
to "keep up with the Joneses", the brand loyalty and mockery of cheaper items
which would form a basis for bullying; it all pissed me off. I also found it really
difficult to express myself and find my own personal style without spending a
fortune. The high-street shops and brands enflamed my bitter teenage elitism,
but independent outlets were often too expensive; so I ended up making my own
clothes, printing on t-shirts and hoodies etc.

Having been relatively naive to it before, I now came face-to-face with the
appalling state of ethics in the fashion industry. The child labour, the poor pay
and atrocious working conditions, the environmental impact; deforestation,
wasteful water usage, harmful chemicals and the big carbon footprint. So the title
of the track is a rally cry against the 'sweatshop'.

From 2001 onwards we ran into lot of bad experiences with our local council
as they often tried to shut local gigs down, this was already teaching us not to
always respect authority. Similarly the perils of the fashion industry began to
introduce me to the nasty side effects of capitalism.

This song is all about exploitation. The opening line, "Where's your respect?
Why bite the hand that feeds you" is my bewilderment at the companies who
treat their own workers with such disdain. The second line introduces the
adverse nature of life for the worker in this environment. Often with factories in

some of the poorest countries, the workers are forced to take on such poorly-paid, back-breaking jobs as there is simply nothing better on offer, and if they were to threaten to leave or try to organise unions they would be very easily disposed of. And there are always more desperate workers for the impassive fat cats to recruit – "Plenty more fingers for you to nibble".

The track ends with one of the most satisfying lines on the whole album to sing. It's the fight-back from the workers. Mistreat us, dispose of us, profit from our exploitation one more time and we shall retaliate.

1 Yes Latin readers, of course we are aware 'non sequitur' is not an adjective …

Brixton, London, UK. January 2019 – Tom Pullen

TODAY WON'T GO DOWN IN HISTORY

You might never meet me
For I am King

And as we march into the storm's eye
I find relief in the rain
I can hide as I lead my army into certain death

Eyes, all of you

Feel Alive

And I wanted you to know
Today won't go down in stone

And I wanted you to know
I never meant for this
Close your eyes

Today won't go down in history
So shut your eyes

Up until the time that this book goes to print, Enter Shikari has only played this track live during one, relatively recent, tour (the ten-year anniversary tour of *Take To The Skies* itself). Which is a bit of a shame, as I think it's one of the few tracks on the album that would sit rather comfortably on any new album we'd create now.

I suppose you could say the song itself was our first expression of an anti-war position. It relays the mental turmoil of a military commander leading his troops into battle and like most of the battles throughout human history, it is a battle that simply won't be remembered or celebrated. Just another parochial encounter that perhaps seemed crucial at the time but, to us now, is of no consequence or interest. I hoped this theme would highlight the absurdity and futility of war.

I try to convey the sheer desperation, hopelessness and claustrophobia of the situation. I imagine, as some higher ranking commander, that I'm about to risk my life, perhaps for a dictator on the offensive or for some strategic geo-political reason, or even, perhaps, without knowing to what end I am fighting for at all, but all the while understanding the broader perspective – the battle is trivial, death is inevitable and that my valour will go unnoticed. It wasn't inspired by a particular historical event, more the plethora of events throughout history that echo this bleak scenario. It's probably one of the most dark and nihilistic songs I've ever written and was inspired by the lofty and privileged position we sit in today, studying history with all its millions of battles, most now consigned to oblivion.

Lyrically, the piece is linked with 'Ok, Time For Plan B', itself a track about the impassioned haste and almost eagerness in which we as humans opt for conflict even before diplomacy, conversation and civility has been exhausted. We hear this allusion in the sombre, regretful line "And I wanted you to know, I never meant for this".

Wrexham, UK. Feb 2016 – Alexey Makhov

RETURN TO ENERGISER

You look like you rented a smile from someone
But you rented the wrong size
Take it back ... you should take it back

Bury it
That's not what you want
'Cos that would grow more
That's not what you want

We still have the element of surprise
Defence shields down

Return to energiser

Wave your bloody white flags
Surrender
Give in

And all hell breaks loose, when you're here

SORRY,
YOU'RE NOT A WINNER

Scratch card glory or waist low pleasure?
Black eyes nose bleeds. Don't look back now
My white abode, do you remember my white abode?

But it's such a thrill, just to find out …

Sorry you're not a winner
With the air so cold and a mind so bitter
What have you got to lose but false intentions and a life so
pretentious?

I sweat, I ache

Please try again. Insert your coin

This was the first offering by the fledgling Enter Shikari and, as we progressed, we've tried multiple times to bury it.

It already felt a bit old when we recorded for a 4-track EP long before the release of *Take To The Skies*, but, as it became a live favourite, we felt including 'SYNAW' on the album was paramount. In a vain attempt to secure it as a non-front line track, we decided to make 'SYNAW' the B-side to 'Ok, Time For Plan B', the first single from the album. Radio, perhaps put off with the loud bulldozing impact of 'Ok, Time For Plan B', had other ideas and only played the B-side; it quickly became apparent that 'SYNAW' had jostled its way to be the lead track.

The track is about nothing more than the nasty trait of brash over-confidence, and the, though maybe immature, still pleasurable act of informing the cocksure when things don't work out in their favour. Like most of my pre-Shikari lyrics, it's mostly nonsense; simple fun with words and images.

The famous claps are just another way to include an audience in a performance. We saw them as similar to gang vocals, human pyramids, playing shows amongst the crowd … just another way to bring everyone closer together.

St Albans. 2004

JOHNNY SNIPER

Rise
Taste the air
Lock and load
Pull the trigger
Climb to new heights
And tell me what you hear …

A whisper from the wind and I can't help but listen
It warns us of disaster and I can't help but wonder
Can anyone hear the same distress call?

So this is a quest to save the world
And he'll always be here for another
Another day, another chance to rescue

This is all I need to feel alive

The crashing of white waves and I can't help but listen
The screaming of the earth and I can't help but …

Hey Johnny! Way to save the world

Wrexham, UK, Feb 2016 · Alexey Makhov

ADIEU

And I long for you to appear
After losing your way across star-riddled skies
To carry you home

I cherish my loss
A gentle reminder that *life is unkind at the best of times*

Look up into the skies

Home could be anywhere when I am holding you

Originally this track was a different beast entirely; far heavier and more angsty, fortified by a fuzzy wall of distorted guitars and high, bellowed vocals. As a song basically about love and loss, it seemed fitting to take the sting out of the original arrangement in order to produce something altogether far more delicate. (Consequently, it still makes me question those that demand our new music to be heavy or "like our original, heavier sound" citing *Take To The Skies* as some apparent benchmark. Did they forget 'Adieu'? 'Johnny Sniper'? 'Interlude 1'? 'Today Won't Go Down In History'? Those folks' memories are either shoddy or extremely selective! Melody and harmony will always be central to everything we do. We ain't a fuckin' death metal band.)

'Adieu' isn't based on any particular personal experience. It is more an homage to the frightening power of love, be it platonic or romantic. It doesn't just celebrate and bask in love's ability to make one feel comforted, ("Home could be anywhere, when I am holding you" being my version of "home is where the heart is") but it also speaks of love's ability to suppress comfort with heartbreak or loss ("Life is unkind at the best of times"). So love, in effect, is a sort of risk. It can bring both security and insecurity, stability and instability.

This is a track that has truly been accepted and owned by our audience. It has been played at countless weddings and funerals and has truly transcended any initial intent I had for it. I really treasure that fact. It is a great feeling to know something I've created has been fostered and utilised, and has gone on to assist so many. It is truly you dear reader, not us, that owns this song.

OK, TIME FOR PLAN B

Let this battle commence, one last time!
(And I hope for your sake, that you're on our side)

Look what you've done to yourself
Yeah you've lost the will to do what's right again

We'll fight like sharks, we'll fight like dogs
We've tried to communicate
But we've got no patience
Let's reclaim this throne
Why should we negotiate?
Let's finish this now!
Let's settle this now, for once and for all

The time has come to think again
Ok, time for *plan B*: This means war!

Everyone freezes and waits for the earth to move
Everyone freezes and waits for the ground to shake

Let's make the earth move
Let's make the ground shake

Essay 1:7 OK, TIME FOR PLAN B

In the commentary for 'Anaesthetist' you'll read about the first protest march I ever went on. However, the second protest I ever went on was the anti-Iraq War march in 2003. A million people took to the streets of London to demand that war was not the answer. It was widely felt at the time that we were being mislead and rushed into a conflict when there was no thorough plan, exit strategy, public appetite, and a lack of confirmed intelligence. It was with this backdrop of pensive sadness and anger that 'Ok Time For Plan B' was written in 2005, just as the war was becoming recognised as a complete failure.

With the publication of the Iraq enquiry (aka the Chilcot Report) in 2016, we had our earlier trepidation confirmed. Sadaam had no weapons of mass destruction and we were dragged into war by the then prime minister, Tony Blair, before diplomacy and peaceful options had been exhausted.[1] This track is also inextricably linked to 'Fanfare Of The Conscious Man'[2] where my frustration with Blair reaches its lyrical peak!

'Ok, Time For Plan B' is a phrase that I hoped would encompass the readiness and apparent eagerness in which countries declare war. But it's not just a song about global and civil warfare, it also depicts the personal too. As a species, humans are often quick to resort to violence when faced with a problem. Perhaps our adrenal glands are too big and our prefrontal cortex too small. Are we still so haunted by our species' more violent, animalistic past?

I'll end on some good news though: violence, both international and small scale has been decreasing now for centuries. Our temperament and ability to live peacefully alongside each other is improving; we *are* evolving.[2]

1 Sir John Chilcot, BBC news http://www.bbc.co.uk/news/uk-politics-36721849 (6th July, 2016)
2 Steven Pinker, *The Better Angels Of Our Nature* (Viking, 2009)

Nagoya, Japan. 2018 – Tom Pullen

THE FEAST

We're trapped in the ribcage of a wildebeest
Come join the feast
Sit down at the head of the table
We'll eat our way out now

The orangutan is quite content, sipping his champagne
The minotaur has lost its cool, it's time to start his reign

Now raise your glass let's make a toast
Let's make an oath
Let's make this carcass fit for a king
Come join the feast

Roll up, roll up, I am your host
The father, the son and the holy ghost
I will not let you escape

I'm swinging from a chandelier
Let's crash the party!

Saarbrücken, Germany, Aug 2015 – Jordan Hughes

KICKING BACK ON THE SURFACE OF YOUR CHEEK

Deck chairs out lads, here's the spot
A spanking panoramic view
The soil here is silk
The air is selective:
"Whose lungs shall I fill with my glorious vapours?
Whose lungs shall I fill with my glory?"
Breathe in, breathe out
Stand tall, stand proud

Taking in all you see
You begin to register cliffs as teeth
And the fucking penny drops
I've been kicking back on the surface of your cheek, all along
…

I'm gonna dive right in your mouth
And cut off your tongue
And hide there forever

Take to the skies, it's time to live

ACID NATION

Huddled in this acid nation
With apprehension

You are expected to gulp down hindrance

This is a celebration of spirit and of mind
When your body's resignation is heard, you can ignore

This is an acid nation
We will persevere
This is an assignation
We will persevere

Feel the rays beat down

Next time you open your eyes
Be thankful the world never wears a disguise
Here's the sun to reveal …

And anyway who cares?
The sun is out
Stare at the sun

This is everything I ever wanted
This feeling's all I need

This piece begins with a criticism of the classic British idiom to have a 'stiff upper lip'; to have self-restraint in expressing emotion – to simply 'bottle it up' and get on with it, in times of adversity or emotional difficulty. In the mid-19th century it became attributed to British people, and in particular those who had the misfortune of being brought up in the single-sex public boarding schools of the Victorian era, where to display emotion was perceived a weakness and discouraged (or even punished).

Today we have a widespread mental health crisis with a tragically under-resourced approach to treatment. With the pressures of the modern world so immense, it is truly amazing how much suffering we are able to endure. I suppose that sums up the main thrust of this piece: "a celebration of spirit and of mind".

"Be thankful the world never wears a disguise" expresses the simple fact that nature never withholds its true state and we too, as a product of nature, shouldn't be expected to disguise ourselves either.

Towards the end of the song the positive visual imagery of the sun and its rays is analogising the relief and connection one feels when one eventually ventilates one's troubles with another human being. To speak about one's hardships or mental demons is to begin the process of emancipation from them. That feeling when you connect with another human, or even just the liberation of communicating with someone, can feel amazing in and of itself.

Cardiff, UK. Feb 2016 – Alexey Makhov

The Zone. Mini-album sleeve by Keaton Henson

KEEP IT ON ICE

I'm biting the blade of your scissors
As the champagne fizzes; keep it on ice
There's plenty more biting to do yet

Words dribble from my mouth
But don't even reach your lungs
So have little hope in penetrating your fucking noodley tangle

St Albans, UK. Aug 2008 – Ian Johnsen

WE CAN BREATHE IN SPACE, THEY JUST DON'T WANT US TO ESCAPE

And what comes next?
A chance to save ourselves?

Imagine magma encrusted in rock
And on the surface of this world
All eyes are on the clock

All our empires, our philosophies
Our practised faiths, our revolutions
Our proud sciences, are but a flicker in one day of the lives of the stars

We can breathe in space they just don't want us to escape

The constellations, yes, all 88 of them
Like the G8, they meet to procrastinate
"Greetings, we are an infant species
Crawling into our own premature decline"
The north star is chairing the meeting
He knows we're spoilt and he's sniggering at our histories

The hollow proposals mean we'll migrate
But they'll bleed us dry until the 11th hour
And when dawn breaks I'll sit and stagnate
With this metric tonne on your shoulders, how do you cope?

Let's prove the stars wrong
We've got to do this

I find it hard to believe that we are alone …

Brixton, London, UK. January 2019 – Tom Pullen

COM

DREA

ERA

MON
DS

St Albans, UK. Summer 2009 – Steve Gullick

Common Dreads. Album sleeve by Dominic Murphy

COMMON DREADS

A heedless and harrowing future is developing
For our generation and generations to come

But as I walk the chartered streets of this familiar oblivion
I recognise nothing but unyielding unconsciousness;
In which we have almost comfortably drowned

It is madness
This normality is madness!

We are clinging to manufactured crippling constraints
We must no longer commute between brand laden homes
And quickly accepted, aimless roams
From our factories of slavery to wars of illusive bravery

We must unite
And we must let the floodgates open

Here tonight I clock a thousand heads
Here to unite through common dreads

Luckily, not even my schooling could cleanse me of the need to write poetry. Yes, I was one of those geeky kids that actually enjoyed writing poetry, even though it seemed to me that my English Literature classes were doing everything in their power to steer me away from writing. To me, most of the syllabus seemed to be made up of the most irksome and unlikable texts that were completely irrelevant to my life and therefore wholly uninspiring. Just how the poetry of Carol Anne Duffy or the novels of Emily Brontë (I'm looking at you, *Wuthering Heights*) could be perceived as magnetising reads for a young teenager, or a successful gateway that would draw the youth into the world of the written word, leaves me dumbfounded.

This was a piece I wrote whilst receiving the cosmopolitan education that was touring our first album worldwide. I wanted to open *Common Dreads* with a stark and clear synopsis; a sharp silhouette of the music and themes that were to follow.

The bulk is performed by Chris' Granddad and Rob's Dad, with occasional help from Rory's young niece. The "we must unite" line is then repeated in a whole host of languages. We did this by utilising the #ShikariFamily around the world and were astounded and touched by the result.

London, UK. Feb 2016 – Alexey Makhov

SOLIDARITY

Here tonight I clock a thousand heads
Here to unite through common dreads

So who's with me?

Something trips inside that's been dormant for a thousand years
Now we can no longer hide the immediacy of these fears

Our names will not be writ on water
And we don't need an ark, no way
One day I know the dam will collapse
And we will be the current

And no the floodgates will open
You cannot hold back the tide

We will sing as one in solidarity
We will swim together
No longer treading water
We're flowing with the tide
And you can taste the night
Don't waste the night
We will sing as one in solidarity
We will sing together now

And still we will be here, standing like statues
The time is now, belt it brothers

Common Dreads is an album that attempts to convince you that all the biggest problems facing us transcend borders, be it poverty and inequality, climate change and resource depletion, racism and sexism, corporate power and debt slavery, nationalism and the military industrial complex, nuclear proliferation and terrorism. All these concepts and structures, directly or indirectly, affect every single citizen who walks upon this floating rock we call Earth.

The concept of 'Solidarity' is the humane response to the realisation of this position, and this track follows the epiphany of finding people power. It's a track about overcoming differences and uniting worldwide as human beings.

I picked water as the metaphorical parallel for the power we wield when united. No thirst can be quenched from a droplet and it is all too easy to suffer the cruel fate of evaporation. But with the might of the vast oceans, a tsunami of change can be achieved.

I've always found water particularly inspiring. Its beauty, its power and, being a city boy, its allure. The British seaside holidays I had growing up stuck with me; I can still hear the delighted shouts of "I can see the sea!" as my family reached the shores of Cornwall or Norfolk. Excursions in my uncle's boat stuck with me too, experiencing the colossal depth and the rich bounty of deep greens and blues that blur from an expanse of water into the horizon when far out at sea.

There are more literary inspirations here too; one example being when I learnt about Thales (the man often regarded as the first western philosopher) who posited that everything was made of water - not as entirely stupid as it first sounds, considering that it was believed everything was made of hydrogen (itself two thirds of water) as recently as the 1920s.

The first mention of water in the track is inspired by a line from the poet John Keats (1795-1821) who, just prior to his death, asked for his tombstone to read 'Here lies One Whose Name was writ in Water.' Many believe this to be him communicating his frustration at such a cruel, early death before gaining wide public acclaim for his work. I wanted to assertively insist that we must and will prevail as a species. As I introduce water as the inspiring substance for the song, I wanted resilience and steadfastness to flow with it: "Our names will *not* be writ on water".

With the line "You cannot hold back the tide" I attempt to stress that this need we all strive for – peace, humanity, equality – are natural phenomena and therefore futile to fight against. A naively optimistic position, perhaps, but our music has always been the music of hope. And this idea is embellished: "no longer treading water, we're flowing with the tide" is a prediction that this future is inescapable.

The track ends with that enduring and formative phrase from *Take To The Skies*, this time presented by a choir - perhaps the definitive musical form with which to broadcast solidarity.

I honestly think the most important concept for social progress today is solidarity: sticking up for the plight of the other, even if their plight doesn't affect you whatsoever. At some point in time you will be part of a minority, or caught in some kind of struggle against a sinister power, and you will long for people to stand by you. This concept is called *reciprocal altruism* in evolutionary terms, and is a key tactic for survival. It has also never been more important than in today's turbulent world.

Nottingham, UK. Feb 2016 – Alexey Makhov

STEP UP

If our own lives aren't directly affected
Then it don't need to be corrected
How fucking cute is our ignorance?
Yeah, we're insidious as they're praying for deliverance
We shelter ourselves from the outcries
We blinker ourselves from the eyesores

But I know we have greatness within us

"We have greatness within us;
Innovative, giving, determined – it's time for the best in us to come out"

Search and you can find imbalance
Seek you can destroy imbalance
And you can change your values
Step up today

Now let me get one thing straight, you know what?
Sometimes I do wish apples were our currency
So your hoarded millions would rot in their vault
Then that'd teach you to lay off the assault
That you're barraging on the lands of the poor
And I know we've all got enough problems of our own
But they're not show stoppers, sitting on our throne
In a home heated by a life unknown to the exploited

And it's so frustrating; the fucking state we're in!

If our own lives aren't directly affected
Then it *does* need to be corrected

"Why is it so many companies built to serve us end up ruling us?"

The opening lines of this piece speak of our depressing ability to shut out suffering when it doesn't affect us. And I speak from personal experience here. This track is not me pointing the finger - it is, once again, an assessment of our species, me included. 'Step Up', in stark contrast with its predecessor, is about when society has a paucity, or a complete absence, of solidarity. When simply getting by is such a struggle that the bigger picture is nothing but a distant blur, or when so wrapped up in riches that the bigger picture is an inconvenience, an eyesore, something that spoils one's isolated happiness.

"Sometimes I do wish apples were our currency, so your hoarded millions would rot in their vaults." It's important to always conduct thought experiments, to see if you believe we are living in the most just and sustainably constructed system, or whether other constructs would bring better results, if for no other reason than it can help clarify the problems of the current system and indicate new solutions or directions that should be worked on. One recurring problem in economics is when those with the most money hoard rather than invest it. So with this line, in my naivety, I'm imagining a currency which, when stashed above a reasonable level, acquires an expiry date.

One critical assessment of humanity would be that we are not squirrels. If you pay attention to squirrels you'll see they are cautious, self-serving animals – they find their seeds and nuts and they hide, store and *hoard* those nuts. They don't tend to cooperate with one another, work together, help one other out. Now I'm told we're substantially more evolved and attuned as a species. We have the ability for complicated cognition, cooperation, logic, compassion and empathy but we often appear to be exceedingly focused on mimicking the squirrel.

JUGGERNAUTS

And I know that we've still got time
But I do not think we're invincible
And I'm thinking that it's a sign
'Cos I do not think we're invincible

Crushing all in its path

Now don't get me wrong, I love what you've done with the place
I just wish we had a chance to help build it
Instead of just moving into this home of disrepair
And expected to work, prosper and then share
Constantly relying on consuming to feel content
But only because we've lost touch with this home that we've spent
Trillions of dollars tainting for our wants, not our needs
And now we're growing tired of planting bleary-eyed seeds

And I'm not saying that we could do better
But given the chance we'd try
We'd dig up the earth's timeworn soil
And fill the trench with greedy eyes

Imagine …

"Back in the day as empires made haste
To colonize, to claim, to control and contain.
We sat patiently in the future, helpless"

Switch. Deep breaths, clench fists
Here comes another Juggernaut!

What the hell will happen now?
I really don't know man!
We'll do what we've always done?
Shut our eyes and hope for the best?
No! We're gonna face this
We'll step out onto the tracks
And stare it right in the face
Thou shall not pass

The idea of community will be something displayed at a museum …

After completing the extensive touring that came with the release of *Take To The Skies*, I began to witness how, around the rest of the world – just as in England – small businesses (and communities in general) were being corroded by corporate power. Companies like Walmart in the U.S. were spreading far and wide with the unstoppable pace and might of a juggernaut.

I felt particularly galvanised to write about the phenomenon after reading *Tescopoly*,[1] a book that presented the overwhelming evidence to show that the supermarket chain Tesco is far from a force for good in the world and instead, *at best*, a cold, ruthless and heartless beast. In response to this, the sentiments introduced in 'Solidarity' are echoed throughout this track with cohesive and steadfast imagery such as "deep breaths, clench fists" and "we're gonna face this, we'll step out onto the tracks".

"Crushing all in its path" is how these colossal businesses often conduct themselves as they expand. Whether it's eliminating local businesses, manipulating planning laws and subverting local councils, or threatening farmers and suppliers while ignoring and endangering the environment.

Much of *Common Dreads* looks at different ways in which market economics has failed us, and is an onslaught of anger at the extensive detrimental effects of capitalism. The negative consequence that seemed to hit me the most regarding supermarket monopolies was the complete disregard for, and subsequent decimation of, local communities, which paved the way for my fear (elucidated at the end of the track) of even losing community as a concept altogether!

The warning is simple, if we stay on our current track of systematically placing profit above people, "The idea of community will be something displayed at a museum". (Though I far from regret this line, it should be mentioned that it has actually been twisted and used against us in the Daily Mail and other right-wing newspapers to attempt to make us out as some kind of detestable and frightening anti-social movement, whereas, of course, that is what the song is directly rallying against.)

1 Andrew Simms *Tescopoly: How One Shop Came Out on Top and Why it Matters* (Constable & Robinson, 2007)

London, UK. Feb 2016 – Alexey Makhov

Australia. Jan 2007

WALL

I'm gonna paste you up
Cover you in wallpaper
Screw shelves into you
And call you a wall

That's all you are to me
Trying to keep people inside
Inside your sordid little house
This is no white abode

You can have skirting board shoes
And plug sockets on your knees
I'll hang a painting on your lip
And put tinsel 'round it at Christmas

Trying to keep people inside, inside your sordid little house

You can't keep us inside much longer pal
We've seen the view from the window …

It's glorious outside
Have you seen the time? Have you seen the tide?
We'll sing all night: we need cohesion

As time keeps moving we keep losing our rights
Freedom is not the choice between what job and what car
You can just look back into history to find corruption and mystery
And if we don't take note we'll wake up in the same boat

Grit your teeth then break the glass
Now sprint and don't look back
Full pelt in to the dense forest
And ask him "what's your thoughts on lionising?
What's your thoughts on the tensions rising?"
Deep in the dense forest

Live At Rock City. Album sleeve by Ian Johnsen

ZZZONKED

Mate, I'm zonked absolutely spent
I think I'm gonna give up my eyes for lent
I'll use my sockets to stock stones instead
And with an icy cold stare, I'll hide bones in your bed

Mate, please accept this invitation, so I can take you away

'Cos there's a one in forty thousand chance
That asteroid Apophis will collide with the earth
In less than 20 years

Roll up for the knees up business

Instead of staring at your Stella desperately for inspiration
Belt up and quiver at your indignation
I ain't saying anything that could be construed as an apology
There's another case study of anthropology
Let's announce embargos and denounce our far foes
Ingrowing egos; a syntax he knows
It's just distance that separates us –
Or are we really all ethnocentrically inclined?

Mate, what the fuck are you going on about?

This is a draconian law, I protest
The herd is rowdy, the squad is vexed

HAVOC A

The Lions are at the door
We ain't taking orders from snakes no more

… Just another day in the Acid Nation
Expected to gulp down hindrance
Hold tight the *real* news networks; they're crucial

NO SLEEP TONIGHT

And I'm thinking what's the deal with the facts that they conceal?
And I'm thinking what's the harm in a bit of rhetoric and charm?

And I can't quite comprehend a beginning or an end
No I can't quite stomach this now

You and me we're gonna take to the skies for common sake
We'll fly amongst the cirrus clouds
Twenty-thousand feet we'll clock the crowds
And from that height we'll leak the lies
And unveil the damaged skies
'Cos we can't quite stomach this

All I'm trying to say is, you're not getting any sleep tonight

The sun and the sea could power us
No longer cower in oil lust
Chernobyl is still a stain
Of the dangers of this game

We'll embark on our great voyage to sun
And we'll be ninety million miles from anything or anyone
What are we waiting for?
Just like the ocean, we won't be pacific anymore
No longer in coexistence with other species, this is flawed …

We live in an increasingly divided and unequal world. Oxfam recently published a study stating that just 62 people own the same amount of wealth as the poorest half of the world's population.[1] Some believe this is perfectly acceptable, that billionaires probably "worked for it" (even though most fortunes are inherited) but do you really think the scale of difference between how hard a labourer works and how hard a billionaire business owner works is in line with the difference in their wealth? The relation between effort and reward is skewed beyond all recognition once we start comparing such vast sums of money. The billionaire would need fifty pairs of arms, never sleep, and have a brain size proportional to a chihuahua's to have his effort/ reward ratio proportional to the labourer's.

Most people are genuinely shocked and angered by othe extent of inequality today, but I think as it becomes more and more extreme we will observe a big change in human social interaction and psychology. A sense of disgust will propagate throughout all areas of society and it will begin to amplify. I believe, in the not too distant future, the 1% will begin to feel a very deep sense of embarrassment as the pressure from the magnitude of inequality becomes so widely despised.

Those who have studied the disparity between rich and poor already feel this sense of revulsion. Hell, even in the rare moments I get to rub shoulders with celebrities and wealthy corporate 'fat cats', I feel no respect or admiration, only a niggling aversion. There's nothing wrong with working hard and earning rewards, but when you acquire more money that you could ever need, whilst surrounded by such vast poverty, there is undeniably a moral duty to redistribute it.

Alright, rant over.

'No Sleep Tonight', like 'Gap In The Fence' to follow, is a reaction to the modern rate of inequality. It is a song about the conscience (or should I say lack of …) of those who prevent progress because there happens to be profit in stasis.

"The sun and sea could power us, no longer cower in oil lust" it is entirely possible for our world to be powered solely by renewable energy.[2] The main stumbling blocks are political, *not* technological. What this means is we have the capability of combating climate change and pollution and making a safer world that runs on clean energy, *but* we are stalling because there are too many people in the energy industry too heavily invested in fossil fuels. And as fossil fuels begin to run out, they will only become more expensive as their scarcity increases, expanding the possible profits for those involved.

In this instance, capitalism is in direct conflict with the safety and future prosperity of our species.

1 *An Economy For the 1%: How privilege and power in the economy drive extreme inequality and how this can be stopped*, Oxfam, (January 2016)
2 Mark Z. Jacobson, *100% Wind, Water and Solar (WWS) All-Sector Energy Roadmaps for Countries and States* (Stanford University Atmosphere/Energy Program, 2015)

GAP IN THE FENCE

I lie here
Staring up at the stratosphere and hoping we're gonna get out of here

And it seems mad
That we're born on the doorstep of squalor and of pedestals

And I lie here
Surrounded by a range of general anaesthetics
To drowse the fact that funding in 'security'
Is not matched by spreading equality

You'll hear us singing …
In the sunlight where you caught us
Plotting the downfall of hoarders

It seems that every gap in the fence
We'll peak, we'll scratch, we'll stretch, we'll grab anything we can

But if we grouped together and made a bigger hole
Not just for our children's hands but for bigger plans
Yeah if we grouped together and made a hole
'Cos I don't know about you but I've gotta get out of here

We live so subserviently
Accepting all normality
Drenched with routine
Doused in the foreseen
And yes, granted we prosper
But the fact that we prosper
Is even taken for granted

HAVOC B

Now let's cause some fucking havoc
The lions are at the door
We ain't taking order from snakes no more

Now we're gonna take a stand
For we are the Grassroots Resistance

Power

All this killing is obscene; shut down the war machine!

ANTWERPEN

Now I was feeling like a total giant!
But now it feels like Silvius Brabo has sliced my hand off
And thrown it in the river

Now I was just doing my job
My feet sink into the bed of the Scheldt
But now my fingers are reeling about with the fishes

I know I'm not making any sense
("No, you're not")
All will be revealed
("Well I hope s-")
All will be revealed if we travel back in time

I've got to rest, it's for the best
To build a nest, to take the quest
To be given just one chance, to be the best

Go forth and re-colonize
It appears the foundations of all our great nations
Are lies and indoctrinations
So if Silvius Brabo collects the hands of giants …
Will you join him?

This track is linked thematically to 'No Sssweat', a track that ends with a threat to bite the fingers off of those who exploit others (an inversion and perversion of the phrase "Why bite the hand that feeds you"). 'Antwerpen' echoes this sentiment by presenting the folk tale of how the Belgian city supposedly acquired its name from the Dutch 'Hand Werpen', literally meaning 'throwing hand':

Silvius Brabo was a Roman soldier who killed a giant called Druon Antigoon. The Scheldt was the river that Druon Antigoon supposedly forced travellers to pay a toll to cross. When they refused or couldn't pay, he would cut off their hand and throw it in the river. When Silvius Brabo faced the giant, in a flash of poetic justice, he severed the giant's hand and threw it into the river. (After which I hope he put his hands on his hips and sassily shouted "see how you like it!")

The last line is a rallying cry to stand up and fight back against the exploitative giants in your life.

Still today in Antwerpen, outside the town hall, you can see the statue of Silvius Brabo throwing the hand into the river.

THE JESTER

"Simmer down ladies and gentlemen
you're acting rather irresponsibly right now, damn you all"

Hold your horses, steady now
'Cos we're floating precariously and therefore furthermore frivolously
On tectonic plates

And everything we stand on
And everything we stand for
Is rather unstable right now

So I think I'll kill some time and have you done medium rare
But I think I'll tease my pallet with some crudités, just to prepare
You see we've had a joker in the pack now for quite some time
So I reckon it's just about time we roast this swine

This is a crock of shit I refuse to be fed
So knuckle down and use your head
Can it sunshine, bottle it up you ponce
Then knock me up a dish with some vol-au-vents
Now I think we should take a leaf from the Romans' book; throw it up
Let's throw it up and start again

Nicely does it now …

Steady …
Hold …
Hold …
(Target locked)

Cop a load of this one

That was great, my compliments to the chef, I'm very satisfied
I'll be sure to dine here again, fine cuisine
The stuffed cheeks were very agreeable
All in all a splendid spread

Brixton, London, UK. January 2019 – Tom Pullen

HECTIC

To the multi-storey car park with our friends
Drinking from a bottle of White Lightning
On top of Marks and Sparks, roof running
Smoking chronic. Hectic

And it seems that nothing now will ever change
And it seems that we're on our own again

We'll convene at mine 3pm to play Sega Megadrive
Golden Axe and Sonic, all day
"Never played it? I'll teach you
Can't hack it? I'll beat you"
That's Pendell making rhymes in the corner
With a litre of the finest Scrumpy Jack
Whilst Pdex pumps out the latest big club track
We'll chip it to Justin's and hit his King Kong
Then we'll gather round the piano for a little sing song

Amongst the gloomy subjects tackled throughout *Common Dreads*, 'Hectic' stands out in that it's a track about the oblivious, carefree, youthful lifestyle that one longs for again upon discovering the 'real world' (a phrase I visit in 'Myopia').

As I was beginning to lose friends to university, jobs and 'life' in general, and the success of *Take To The Skies* meant that touring schedules had me away from home for more than a year, I wrote this song about what now seemed a lost, breezy and untroubled Halcyon era.

"The multi-storey car park" "on top of Marks and Sparks" are two spots just off of St Peter's Street in St Albans where we used to hang out drinking cheap cider and getting up to no good.

"That's Pendell making rhymes in the corner …" Matthew Pendell is an old friend of mine who I'd often make more light-hearted music with, be it in the ironic metal band 'The JBM' or under the guise of the comedy duo 'Matty P & Tony G'.

"Whilst Pdex pumps out …"Pdex is Rory's elder brother, a Drum 'N Bass DJ whose records were a big influence on us growing up.

Budapest, Hungary. Aug 2016 – Jordan Hughes

FANFARE FOR THE CONSCIOUS MAN

Each nation used to provide its country with security
With factories providing arms for their country
Now multinational companies compete in the arms trade
To serve any customer, maximising the money to be made

So just as farms compete to provide fruit for other countries
So people can live to enjoy the taste of nature
National warehouses compete to provide arms around the world
To aid death and all hell unfurled

Our gracious queen should grasp her crown
And take a good fucking swing at Blair and Brown
For leading her country into illegal warfare
And trying to pass it off like we're doing 'cos we care

"Now pre-emptive wars are a redemptive cause"
I've never heard such nonsense under international laws
We think we have the right to enforce 'democracy'
When we're weakening ours everyday; what a hypocrisy

We'll be together against this
We'll be forever against this

Fuck man, I just woke up to a land where killing is part of every day
And every mind in this intelligent species
Is led blinded into the battlefield
Like it's natural for us to break instead of build
Unity's intrinsic, the only cause worth fighting for
All religions, colours and creeds

Now, we are the world and we are the people

And we *will* be heard

ALL EYES ON
THE SAINT

22nd of June, 209AD. A crowd gathers:

Oh they fucking love a good beheading
And as St Alban's head rolled down the hill
The crowd stood still, 'cos what they just saw
It petrified them to the core

As the executioner raised his as his axe
I swear the saint smiled

Roman Verulamium, cathedral city
All eyes on the saint

Our city with its beautiful history
Is being diluted
But we will not let go. No we won't
Now get a grip on your roots boy
Don't let go

And it's cold outside

As the executioner swung his lead
His eyes popped right out his fucking head
Not worthy to see the ancient moment
The making of the first British martyr

Here lies truth, where I stand

So where St Alban's head came to rest, after the kill
Fresh water sprung up from the ground
At the bottom of what's now 'Holywell hill'

Tribalism. Mini-album sleeve by Ian Johnsen

TRIBALISM

Shikari was a third generation Aztec
His tribe accepting human reality
It was the basis of their ability to sustain with humble tranquility
But civilisations encouraged religions which in turn introduced depravity
And that was as big a realisation as when my boy Newton discovered gravity
'Cos it transformed the way we bounce about on a daily basis
Not content with a doubt about the knowledge of who's up there
Quick! Give him a name, a trident and a chair
What happened to wonder?
Why can't we accept we're not capable of thunder?
So we welcome the lies with open arms
And we turn into suckers when they turn on the charm

You're trying to run us all into the ground
To be swallowed by the soil and trapped by the rain
In your concrete garden of falseness
You shout through our speakers and we don't turn them off
'Cos trapped in silence it's tougher
But this time we'll turn the speakers off

And we won't stay silent, we'll make as much noise as we can

And I ask what's a thought without a voice to voice it?
It's just a thought

We will shout our heads off
We won't stop until you hear
We won't stop until you trip up upon yourselves

The original affluent society
Floating free of capitalistic anxiety
But all that has survived now is the pack vibe
But the catch is dogs don't eat other dogs
We're able animals employed by criminals in this cannibalistic society
Where we scrimp and save just to behave with the upmost propriety

We won't stay silent

Preston, UK. Aug 2010 – Shirlaine Forrest

THUMPER

Axiomatic subject matter, executed with absolute lucidity

We can't keep deferring action
Only surviving by the skin of our teeth

We're sick of the same old story
Tonight the motionless must vacate
So we can accelerate out of a stagnant society

**We will, we will never be sane
In an unsane system**

Keep the tempo up, keep the pressure on
Someone take the first step, be brave, cave in

"Okay, I admit it, we are totally lost"
Imagine that! And then they'd say ...

*"We've lost the movement, we've lost the beat
We got so tied up in making a profit
That we choked when we realised what was at our feet"*
We're all made of the same dark matter
It's intrinsic that we rise to our feet

We'll start a movement
We'll start a beat ...

FLASH OF COL ERA

FLOOD
OUR

Sweden, December 2018 – Tom Pullen

Destabilise. Single sleeve by Ian Johnsen

DESTABILISE

Today for the very first time
We started planning out the ultimate crime
Locking together to destroy this cold stasis
Rory C, what's your thesis?
"I don't fucking believe this!"
Institutions are established and invested
Pause to ask "are they tried and tested?"
No; just force-fed and digested
It's about time we damn contested

You can't stain us
You can't contain us
You can't destabilise, divide or label us

Now they're cracking under pressure from our force
'Cos we know; we don't belong here
And we're rising through the stubborn assault course
But we're stuck in the middle

Our minds our dormant and static
Don't ever respect conventional thought without reason
We need to fucking erupt!

Corrupted fucking tyrants instigating violence
In sporadic discordance we'll find maximum assurance

This is the calm before the storm
One last siege to break the norm
So I can lie here on the floor
Beside *you*

No one owns:
The oceans
The mountains
Us

We **all** inherited this world
We need to fucking erupt 'cos this earth is ours

Quelle Surprise. Single sleeve by Ian Johnsen

QUELLE SURPRISE

Analysis of the human race in 2011AD …

We've got the technology to move forward
We've got the knowledge and the means to build upstream
We've got the technology to go faster
We've got the passion and the talent to make this real

We're so fucking adaptable, controvertible
Ducking and weaving from the truth
If it adds weight to the content of our pockets
We'll sit and stagnate with banks and use rockets
To oversee that it's our bottom line
That gets carried to the high seas
Well, quelle fucking surprise
If you stand for nothing
You will fall for anything

We're aware they're trying to take away our dreams
We're aware they're trying to take away our means

You are not going to take away our dreams
You are not going to take away our means

SYSTEM ...

There was a house in a field on the side of a cliff
And the waves crashing below were just said to be a myth
So they ignored the warnings from the ships in the docks
Now the house on the cliff is the wreckage on the rocks

Nothing could fix the building's flawed foundation
The scaffolding and stilts were the laws and legislation
This house was doomed, but they didn't care
They'd invested in the system that was beyond repair

When I was little ...
I dressed up as an astronaut and explored outer space
I dressed up as a superhero and ran about the place
I dressed up as a fireman and rescued those in need
I dressed up as a doctor and cured every disease

It was crystal clear to me back then that the only problems that I could face
Would be the same problems that affect us all
But of course this sense of common existence
Was sucked out of me in an instance
As though from birth I could walk but I was forced to crawl

So this is such an exciting time to be alive
Our generations got to fight to survive
It's in your hands now, whose future?

Our future

I wanted to start this album in a similar fashion to *Common Dreads*, with a portion of spoken word poetry. I believe with spoken word you can convey a sense of urgency and honesty better than with melodic or shouted vocals and, as this album opens with this rather dark and stark warning, I decided to perform it myself on this occasion.

I felt the most fitting metaphor for our general cultural and economic paradigm was that of a house built precariously at the top of a cliff, with the sea slowly but surely eroding the base of the precipice. This erosion represents the plethora of problems that are exacerbated within our current system.

At any one time, it seems as if there's a whole host of crises playing out; whether that's the depletion of the earth's natural resources or pollution, deforestation, soaring debt, violence, poverty, crime, migration and the refugee crisis, species extinction and habitat destruction ... the list goes on. These crises are all amplified by the ultimate crisis, one that will only exacerbate all the others: climate change.

"The scaffolding and stilts" that represent the "laws and legislation" ... these are the quick fixes and short term attempts to restrain or conceal the inevitable collapse of society. They're the patchwork and stitching of holes in a broken fabric. When it is, in actual fact, the weak fabric itself that is the problem. We need to design and construct a new society to eradicate the root causes of our current failings. Revisiting the metaphor, we need to build a stable and secure house, away from the cliff edge!

It seems as though we grow up with an urge to create and explore, and to help and care for each other. To collaborate and work together. But all these things become secondary within this system as the basic needs of sustenance and shelter necessitate the acquisition of wealth. With the (currently) prevailing neoliberal, 'dog-eat-dog' worldview, we are pitted against each other in a race that is rigged in favour of the rich. It's almost rather astonishing that we *still* see such vast amounts of humanity, volunteerism and altruism throughout our societies, when there is no systematic reward for this behaviour. This track is heavily inspired by The Zeitgeist Movement, a source of consistent inspiration over the years and a goldmine of perspective and logical thought.

North American tour 2013. Poster by Ian Johnsen

... MELTDOWN

It's your future
And this is gonna change everything; System meltdown

Stand up. How we gonna get through this alive?
It's not too late. How we gonna get out this alive?
Countries are just lines, drawn in the sand

Inside this sick foundation
We've had the realisation
We've had the revelation;

Fuck all borders and fuck all boundaries
Fuck all flags and fuck nationalities

You've got to give us a chance before we reach the system meltdown
Countries are just lines, drawn in the sand with a stick

We begin to learn to smile again
Start to walk that extra mile again
'Cos I know that we are one

Fear begins to vanish when we realise
That countries are just lines, drawn in the sand with a stick

With this album, I began to include increasingly frank and assertive statements within my lyrics. This wasn't really a conscious decision, though I think having found myself in a position where I had a direct influence on people (especially young people) I felt a sense of responsibility to make sure my writing was honest and positive. I also recall being spurred on by the long-standing culture of art and literature providing a reflection of society, not just offering an escape from it. This is an age-old debate that as far as I'm aware started publicly (at least) right back with Wagner and Dvořák and still draws blood today. Myself, being typically diplomatic (my Myers-Briggs personality type is INFP or "the mediator") would say there is room *and* need for both, but I would add the small caveat that, in a particularly corrupt and unequal society, I personally feel more comfortable offering the reflection rather than the fantastical, as it would be remiss of me to remain silent about matters of such moral weight.

Straight off the bat, I begin this album with the frankest of declarations: "Fuck all borders, fuck all boundaries, fuck all flags and fuck nationalities". Always dive in at the deep end, dear reader.

Nation states create a cosmic blindness – a blinkered view that presents our globe as a scattered and detached mess of foreigners, of migrants, of 'the other'. A call for 'national pride' is extremely effective in silencing criticism from subjects, as it triggers an emotional fear of being branded a traitor and the instinctive need to feel 'part of the tribe'.

After writing this song I've since found there to be an extremely rich history of condemnation of nationalism and the base, barbaric behaviour it inspires. The dismissal of the border, the flag and the nation state, and the ugly sociology they enable, is a common position that appears in the work of many of the world's greatest thinkers. When writing the lyric, I was inspired by Einstein's quote 'Nationalism is an infantile disease. It is the measles of mankind'; John Lennon's 'Imagine', 'Imagine there's no countries' and the original badman, Socrates, 'I am not an Athenian or a Greek, I am a citizen of the world', but, at the time, I was unaware of the wealth of other great minds who also lent their words to the this grand rebuke. From H.G Wells', 'Our true nationality is mankind' to Oscar Wilde's 'Patriotism, the virtue of the vicious'; from Seneca's 'I am not born for one corner; the whole world is my native land.' to Arthur Schopenhauer's brilliantly acidic 'Every miserable fool who has nothing at all of which he can be proud, adopts as a last resource pride in the nation to which he belongs; he is ready and happy to defend all its faults and follies tooth and nail, thus reimbursing himself for his own inferiority'.

Almost every human worth listening to over the millennia has had something damning to say about the perils of the nation state. I do not claim to add anything of note to these wise sentiments, I just hope my modern and slightly more curt echoing has in the least, encouraged further reading and thinking.

SSSNAKEPIT

Come and join the party leave anxieties behind
When the weight of all the world is pushing down

Nah nah nah cut this tension mate it's too much

Situation volatile, seriously hostile
Breadwinners, soul searchers
Fear merchants, seeking
Brightly coloured, no use for camouflage
When you're venomous and willing to sabotage
We're just a group of your white blood cells
Fighting off parasites
We're your system mechanics
Trying to fix this machine

What's the one thing that has:
More speed
More strength
And goes deeper than us?

A Nuclear Submarine

Ah come on just open the door!
Knocked off my feet by the back draft
Brought back to earth
Oxygen clears my head
And I just gotta say:
You're not gonna believe this. You can't perceive this
This is like nothing you've seen before
But lucky for you this is an open door

Come and join the party leave anxieties behind
When the weight of all the world is pushing down
Down on your shoulders
Just push right back

They're well prepared but they forgot one thing

We're nice guys …

… Until we're not

Essay 3:3 SSSNAKEPIT

The 'sssnakepit' is that unpleasant hole or dead end we all find ourselves in from time to time, where nothing seems to be going our way. The song is about addressing those slumps, reaching out to others, immersing yourself in all that is positive in your life, and hauling yourself back out.

"Knocked off my feet by the back draft, brought down to earth"

It is with sudden vigour that you can find yourself in this dark pit of bad luck and distress, but it is with a clear head that you can clamber back out and "push right back".

'Sssnakepit' is a celebration of companionship, openness, compassion and perseverance.

Manchester, UK. Feb 2016 – Alexey Makhov

SEARCH PARTY

I know that we're gonna repeat history unless we sort this out
I know that we've gotta find something new

Now my crew is six thousand million strong
But we're not learning from
A history of conflict and violence
And ownership and the power to silence
Retracing all our steps, we sent out the set back search party
To locate the barriers that locks us down
The Phenakistoscope is spinning
Flashbacks to your beginnings
The repetition that you found

All hands on deck
We've gotta scrub these fuckers out

ARGUING WITH THERMOMETERS

This is an expedition into the Arctic tundra
This is a sickening mission, just to spoil and plunder

That's the sound of another door shutting in the face of progress
They'll plant their flags in the sea bed, Shackleton is rolling in his grave

Yeah, we're all addicted to the most abused and destructive drug of all time
And I ain't talking about class A's
That business is minuscule when compared
And just like any addict desperate to get his next fix
We resort to committing crimes to secure our next hit

"You know there's oil in the ice
You know there oil in my eyes
You know there's blood on my hands
Yeah, we're all addicted, we're all dependent"
That's a maniac stand point, a psychotic outlook

So let me get this straight:
As we witness the ice caps melt
Instead of been spurred into changing our ways
We're gonna invest in military hardware to fight for the remaining oil
That's left beneath the ice?
What happens when it's all gone?
You haven't thought this through have you boys …

We'll take you down. Stand your ground

Yeh back to the drawing board boys
Accept nothing short of complete reversal, dig deep

Our modern, energy-intensive lives have been powered by Earth's natural resources; oil, coal and gas. These resources took hundreds of thousands of years to form, but are being polished off in no time at all and, as if the looming exhaustion of these resources isn't enough of a worry, in recent decades it has been confirmed that this way of producing energy directly affects our global climate. We are no longer just one of many species coexisting on one planet; we are now a species so powerful, so audacious and so brazenly self-serving that we directly influence and transform our climate without hesitation. In doing this we ruin habitats and ecosystems, and threaten yet more species with extinction. This is nothing other than interspecies 'betrayal' and is a subject I expand on in the song 'Myopia'.

'Arguing With Thermometers' is a piece about the evidently limitless insanity of energy companies in the lengths they go to to ensure profit, whilst knowingly causing measurable damage to our shared life-support system: Earth.

The track embarks from the Arctic, one of the few remaining fossil-fuel-rich places on Earth untouched – or should I say *unspoiled* – by energy companies. (Though recently they have been fighting to claim various parts of the region as their own in order to drill. "They'll plant their flags, in the sea bed".) What *should* be a protected sanctuary of natural beauty in international waters has become at best a political bargaining chip, and at worst something to stoke the fires of old national rivalries as companies hustle and bustle to lay claim.

I spend some time comparing our dependency on fossil fuels to an addict's reliance on drugs. This feels fitting due to the tunnel vision of dependency, the complete dismissal of logic and refusal or disregard of all negative effects of the drug.

Energy companies even go to the extent of offering large sums of money to scientists in order to promote climate pseudo-science and media distortion on the subject. They do this whilst also lobbying government to halt any legislation (or as they would probably call it 'government interference') on their 'rights' to our shared resources. It seems to me that to promote misinformation around climate change should truly be now considered a crime against humanity (and all other impacted organisms!).

Of course this draws another sad parallel with drug addiction; "we resort to crimes to secure our next hit" whereby the addict will go to any length to get the drug they need. People are paid to lie and obscure evidence in order for big oil companies to continue their addiction; their racketeering.

These are the people who are *arguing with thermometers*. Arguing with the monumental amount of evidence that proves anthropogenic climate change.

To stop catastrophic climate change, we need to force energy companies to switch off and retract their drills. We need to tell them to leave 80% of fossil fuel reserves in the ground. Unfortunately the realisation that we have to make a seismic shift immediately or future generations will be forced to fight for energy capabilities, whilst at the same time dealing with the disasters presented from catastrophic climate change is something that is not on the minds of shareholders. Such a shift would mean re-building entire energy infrastructures, which costs time and money. Things that seemingly no one is willing to give up. Let's be blunt; energy companies are motivated to do all in their power – be it legal or otherwise – to ensure they continue unstirred with their current profit mechanisms, for the benefit of their shareholders. Or, to use what I believe to be one of the most dangerous phrases ever invented, to do all they can to maintain 'business as usual'.

STALEMATE

Previous wars made millionaires out of billionaires
Today's wars make trillionaires out of billionaires
Tomorrows wars will fuel generations of hate

I'm losing my grip on reality I cannot simply agree that we are civilised
Acting like this earth is infinite, it's a chess board of lies
That will generate stalemate

So yes, I've gone to the hills again
So yes, I've gone away

Money is made when bombs are dropping in Afghanistan
When white phosphorous falls in Palestine
Whoring weapons at a record pace
Arming anyone who wants a taste, of disgrace

Oh so I've drifted away in disbelief
And I'll live out this fantasy

I'll live this fantasy …

Stalemate *noun.* a situation in which further action or progress
by opposing or competing parties seems impossible.
ORIGIN C18: from obs. *stale* (from Anglo-Norman Fr. *estale* 'position',
from *estaler* 'be placed') + MATE².

Some wars are won and some wars are lost. Some wars are abandoned. Some
people die and some people are left scarred. What is *certain* to be forever present
in war is hatred and misery. An endless cycle of death, revenge, death, 'justice',
pain, death, revenge, death …

Nothing will change unless a social system is designed that negates the reasons
for war.

Most wars fought today are for the acquisition of resources or land. The system
we have right now encourages war and, like a bystander in some kind of global
school playground fight, stokes the fire from the sidelines.

"Whoring weapons at a record pace, arming anyone who wants a taste"

Nations will arm either (or even both) side of a conflict, the acquisition of profit
trumping any determined ethics. Persuading opponents to resolve things peacefully
won't reap anywhere near as large a financial reward as selling weaponry.

Brixton, London, UK. January 2019 – Tom Pullen

GANDHI MATE, GANDHI

Now I don't know about you, but:

I don't think …
The primary purpose of your life, of my life and the entirety
Of the human race
Is just to blindly consume to support a failing economy and a faulty system
Forever and ever until we run out of every resource
And have to resort to blowing each other up to ensure our own survival

I don't think …
We're supposed to sit by idle while we continue to use a long outdated system
That produces war, poverty, collusion, corruption,
Ruins our environment and threatens every aspect of our health,
And does nothing but divide and segregate us

I don't think …
How much military equipment we're selling to other countries,
How many hydrocarbons we're burning,
And how much money is being printed and exchanged
Is a good measure of how healthy our society is

But I do think …
I can speak for everyone when I say:
We're sick of this shit

Time to mobilise, time to open eyes
We are not a quiet pocket of resistance
This is real and we cannot afford to fail
Act with persistence

"I am the established order, respect me and fear me"
Fuck you, we hold no respect and when tomorrow comes
We're gonna stamp on your head

**"See if we keep them silent; then they'll resort to violence;
And that's how you criminalise change."**

Yabba dabba do one son, we don't want your rules
Who you fooling son?
We got all the tools we need to build a whole new system,
To correct these flaws
"Yeh like what?"
I've already listed them
"You're a communist! You're a fucking utopianist!"
There come the emotive labels but their attempt just fails
'Cos man we're so far out your comfort zone

We stop, think, begin to revive
Put the call out to the front line. Get the message out to the contact squad;
Transmit emergency frequencies

The jigsaw starts to build, piece by piece
Open their minds, transmit emergency frequencies

This song was written at the beginning of 2011, about six months before the Occupy Movement began, and focuses on many of the same problems Occupy communicated so succinctly and so widely.

One of Occupy's main points was a beautifully simple, but drastically important one: you cannot have infinite growth on a finite planet. Developed nations currently consume over three planet's worth of resources. If everyone on Earth lived like - for example - U.S. citizens, Earth's population would require 4.5 times the resources provided by one planet.[1] Obviously, this is a hideously ill-conceived way to live.

Furthermore, the only type of growth our economic system values is the market value of goods and services over time. The success of our economy isn't just evaluated in growth; our economy is completely *dependent* on it.

One way that growth is achieved is though cyclical consumption, which means we must constantly produce goods to ensure sales to create wealth to produce more goods to ensure sales to create wealth to produce more goods to ensure sales to create wealth to … (you get the picture: 'cyclical'), and the best way to ensure the cycle perpetuates is to ensure that the goods are of sufficiently low quality as to need regular replacement ('planned obsolescence', in short).

It does not take a genius to work out that this plan is dramatically short-sighted and completely unsustainable. Once our planet is factored into this blinkered system we realise that we're running an unbalanced budget that can only end with bankruptcy. (A little extra irony can be tasted when we consider that the word 'economy' derives from the Greek, 'oikonomia' which means 'household management'. It appears our collective household, Earth, is being severely mismanaged.)

I expand further with a comment on the foolishness of using Gross Domestic Product (GDP) as measurement of human welfare and social progress.[2] Foolish not only because it ignores our health, sociology and ecology, but also in that so much money is moved around by the upper 5% that the rest is barely negligible. GDP treats the earth like a business that is about to close. You've all seen those high street shops with *"everything must go!"* in the window. We judge our economy purely by the amount of trade taking place and ignore social welfare.

After this rushed analysis of our shared predicament (broadsheet newspapers are often quick to dismiss politically-inspired lyrics as being overly terse or simplistic – I'll remember to write an in-depth two hour Opus next time, guys) I venture to describe the relationship between protesting groups and the status quo, or the Activist and the State.

"See if we keep them silent then they'll resort to violence and that's how you criminalise change."

As a populace, if you feel disempowered, forgotten or excluded - as is so often the case when your only frolic with democracy is a vote every four or five years - it's easy to become angry. Now, anger is a great motivator but if your qualms are ignored, anger will cloud and engulf logic. Helplessness often allows violence to become a default reaction and of course, the State welcomes that, because the State knows exactly how to deal with violence.

So much of this song is about our relationship with outrage, with fury, with exasperation. The title itself was a phrase we'd say to each other when getting frustrated in the studio … an abbreviated evolution of, 'calm down mate, remember the teachings of Gandhi. What would *he* do?'. We thought it would be quite funny to make this song of peace extra heavy and frenzied –, as far from Gandhi's demeanour as possible – whilst still being an Enter Shikari song.

The name calling – "you're a communist", "a fucking Utopianist" – is a sly dig at those who have criticised or dismissed Shikari's politics by simply attempting to label them. In debate, a surefire way of recognising your opponent is losing is when they assign labels to you, trying to put you in a philosophical box that they can then understand and attack. A neat confluence of *ad hominem* and 'Straw Man' fallacy.

1 '*Living Planet Report*, 2010' - World Wildlife Fund, the Zoological Society of London and the Global Footprint Network
2 There are many alternatives now being developed, proposed and used, such as the 'Genuine Progress Indicator', 'Gross National Happiness', 'Happy Planet Index', 'Better Life Index' and 'Human Development Index'.

European tour 2014. Poster by Ian Johnsen

WARM SMILES DO NOT MAKE YOU WELCOME HERE

And with these humble tools we can trigger any emotion we choose
But we'll just settle to pump out repeated relics, diluted with time
You see the airways are clogged up, but the fickle, they lap it up
They need to be drowned in condiments and left to ponder sense

Warm smiles, they do not make you welcome here

Snap back to reality, the turbulence is blowing us from side to side
But no matter how hard you try
Surrounded by cannon fodder
Inundated with stagnant sounds

Transformation: in progress …

… Transformation: complete

Lightning strikes; a flash flood of colour
I can't stand the heat

Musicians can sometimes forget that music exists as a way to express emotion … a way of relaying experience or, indeed, escaping it. To make music is to share a gift and an almost sacred, timeless method of communication. With today's dominant culture of consumerism, popular music could honestly be mistaken for a commodity rather than an art form. With such a varied pallet of possibilities at a composer's disposal, it's frustrating to see music created purely as a means to make money, often resulting in 'product' or 'content' that is meretricious, recycled or soulless.

I like to think that Enter Shikari have always lived somewhere within the small no-man's-land between popular music and the underground, with equally solid footing with the vanguard and the conventional. From that vantage point I've witnessed artists from both of these worlds pollute the airwaves with tawdry, vapid offerings.

Generally speaking, and with very few 'specialist' outliers, mainstream media outlets can only give airtime to the unchallenging, under the belief that 'maintaining market share' of audience requires 'offending' as few people as possible, and as we all know nothing offends an 'audience' more than expressions of genuine emotion <rolls eyes>. This creates a state where music is purposely made to be comfortable or *middle-of-the-road* in order to achieve widespread support.

Heaven forbid we introduce the listener to music they haven't heard before or don't yet understand! It is as though ignorance is rewarded with the yet further broadcasts of the familiar.

Where music is homogenised, lyrical content is also often rendered ineffectual or (maybe even worse) socially and morally weak.

Socially conscious lyrics are few and far between amidst the ongoing current fashion for the glorification of violence & misogyny, the glamorisation of greed & narcissism, or the parade of masculinity & tribalism (pick your genre, everyone's complicit, from hardcore to pop, from metal to hip-hop, from 'EDM' to indie).

As a personal response to this, *A Flash Flood Of Colour* is precisely what I tried to compose with our third album. We wanted to make sure variation of texture, melody, rhythm and emotion was our mission statement.

I leave it to you, dear reader, to assess whether we achieved such heights.

A Flash Flood Of Colour. Album sleeve by Paul Blundell

Nottingham, UK. Feb 2016 – Alexey Makhov

PACK OF THIEVES

Here behind those eyes there is something you should know

Change cannot be subject to conditional falls
'Cos we're squatting in a system that consistently stalls
Don't be fooled into thinking that a small group of friends
Cannot change the world, that's the only thing that ever has

Stand up

Behind those eyes we reach through their callous disguise
Into fortresses where they fabricate whitewash and lies
We're all fooled into living with a small pack of thieves
That distort the world, that's what this antique structure creates

We are all connected
We are all collected here
Now change the world

We blast behind those eyes
Smash through to the cortex
Gut-wrenching business
Caught off guard
Not psyched for the vortex
This can't be real …

HELLO TYRANNOSAURUS, MEET TYRANNICIDE

'Ello Tyrannosaurus, meet Tyrannicide
You haven't read your history have you? Just regurgitated lies
And everything taught to you; that no man is too tall
You can grow but remember; empires always fall …

We're not your subjects
You're not our king
Nature is the only dictator
That I respect and obey

You don't invent
You don't create
Now's our chance to irradiate

"We will torture we will slaughter in your name
We will occupy and we will invade
We will silence and suppress without blame
We will rape, steal, destroy all you made"

Concrete eye contact
Dig your nails into your palms
'Ello Tyrannosaurus

CONSTELLATIONS

Packing the last few shirts into a bloated suitcase
Last glimpse of comfort and the ticking clock face
I swear those hands move faster everyday
I'm more confused than ever but I don't beg or prey
'Cos the sparkling light from the morning sun
Is all we should need to feel one

I reach the station with just minutes to spare
Glance at my watch, time's going faster these days I swear
Eyes focus up now to the train timetable board
There's only two platforms to be explored
And it's then that I admit it to myself
That I am lost, so lost
But you're the constellations that guide me

There's a train at 12; destination disaster
It's running on time, as time runs faster
On platform 2 its destination sustainability
It's delayed though, it was supposed to arrive at 11:50
Platform 1 it says stand behind the yellow line
But I sit on the platform edge and just gaze at the time

My mind wanders back to our oblivious existence
I'm all choked up now with the threat of distance
As the train bound for disaster chokes up to the station
I don't board it 'cos I decide it's the wrong destination
But the train bound for sustainability is nowhere to be seen
And I am lost, so lost, where are the constellations that guide me?

And then I realise that …
We need to use our own two feet to walk these tracks
And we have to squad up and we have to watch each other's backs
With forgiveness as our torch and imagination our sword
We'll untie the ropes of hate and slash open the minds of the bored
And we'll start a world so equal and free
Every inch of this earth is yours all the land and all the sea
Imagine no restrictions but the climate and the weather
Then we could explore space, together, forever …

When we take a step back, the seemingly overwhelming problems we face today can often be viewed with much more clarity.

As a civilisation we find ourselves at a fork in the road and every major decision we make edges us closer down one path or the other (to what I label in this track as the destinations of 'Sustainability' and 'Disaster').

But, let's face it, roads are a bit cliché.

Trains have played a big part of my life. Be it commuting throughout London, travelling to see friends around the UK, or crossing countries and continents while touring. I've been in fits of laughter on a train; I've been swallowing back tears on a train. Trains felt like the most personal and honest mode of transport for me to attempt to achieve poetry in this piece, and indeed they're hopefully nowhere near as stale a metaphor as 'roads' or 'paths'.

Travelling by metaphorical rail also ensured my protagonist had to endure waiting for delayed and cancelled trains – an experience that may be unfamiliar if you are from Japan or any other country where the trains run like clockwork; but for those who *have* experienced this frustration, I felt it was a far more romantic way of expressing the lack of control we have in carving out our collective future.

I hope that the stress of packing, of leaving home (dragging oneself from the gravitational force of loved ones), the panic of rushing, the uncertainty of not knowing whether your transport is running … Without wishing too much of a hard time on you, dear reader, I hope the heightened emotions experienced in these situations will be relatable.

It is in these fraught moments that we long for guidance. Be it from parents, siblings, guardians, friends, Gods, art, philosophy, music. Wherever. We yearn for the answers. We ache for reassurance and empathy. One's own constellations are one's intertwined network of influences, mentors and support: those you love and those you respect. But occasionally that network will be unavailable to you, and you'll have to face your difficulties alone. I felt this was apparent when it comes to the bigger picture, too.

Humans have a great penchant for passing the buck. We assume others will step up to the plate for us, allowing us to withdraw to a safe distance. In psychology this is called the 'bystander' effect, or more specifically 'diffusion of responsibility' where we assume others will act, failing to realise the very others we cite may also be making that same assumption.

So 'Constellations' last verse is all about being bold and is possibly my favourite Shikari 'call to arms': to harness self-love and self-respect, to be courageous and to fight for the change you wish to see in the world, armed with forgiveness and imagination, two of the great driving forces for social progress.

I am, of course, drawing influence here from Gandhi's oft-quoted 'be the change you wish to see in the world', and also from the American theologian Reinhold Niebuhr's serenity prayer 'God, grant me the serenity to accept the things I cannot change, Courage to change the things I can, And wisdom to know the difference'. I wasn't brought up in a particularly religious household, but I remember this being framed on a wall at home. It would also be remiss of me not to mention one specific influence for the last verse; the great comedian and social commentator Bill Hicks and his famous 'it's just a ride' speech. If you are not aware of him, please do indulge yourself, post haste!

London, UK. Feb 2016 – Alexey Makhov

THE PADDINGTON FRISK

To be strung up on a leafless tree
Where everything dies and nothing grows
Hanging like moulding fruit
One last dance whilst you decompose

On come the Paddington spectacles
A black plague over all I admire
A vegetable breakfast, a hearty choke
Seems like the whole world conspired

But there stood a man
He was cut up, distraught and cold
But amongst the wreckage of his ribcage
His heart still thudded as he said:

"I regard myself as a soldier, though a soldier of peace
I know the value of discipline and truth
I must ask you to believe me when I say …"

No matter if it all backfires
No matter if it all goes wrong
We got to get ourselves together
We've sat still for far too long

Now this ain't over yet; as far as I can see, we've only just begun …

This song is composed of various colloquialisms from medieval England. I first came across the phrase 'the Paddington frisk' in a book about the colonisation of Australia, and this introduced me to the marvellous array of what historians call 'plebeian wit': the brilliantly dark humour of the medieval lower classes.

In the 1700s at Tyburn (a village in London located around what is now Paddington / Edgware Road / Marble Arch), hangings were very popular with the public. One way you can tell is by the sheer amount of slang on record to do with the practice. The spasms and violent shaking of limbs that occurred as a person choked to death was said to be comparable to a dance and labelled 'the Paddington frisk'.[1]

The 'leafless tree' was of course the wooden gallows used. I thought this was such a great sardonic use of the word *tree*, something which is synonymous with giving life, but in sharp contrast *this* wooden structure aided only death.

Other bits of beautifully dark medieval banter were 'the Paddington spectacles', which was the bag or blindfold that was placed over the head of the accused,[2] and the pun 'vegetable breakfast, a hearty choke' (to non-native-English speakers, if you drop your H's – as cockneys do – you get the vegetable, artichoke). A couple more terms I couldn't quite fit in, but are equally as ingenuous, include 'to ride a horse foaled by an acorn' to describe the hanging, and the bleak but frank 'a man hanged will piss when he cannot whistle'.

Often, looking back into history gives you a boost of optimism. Regardless of how terrible things may seem now, they were almost certainly worse at any other time throughout history. Being wrongly accused of a crime and sentenced to death could have been just one of many available misfortunes to come your way had you lived in 18th-century London. The hanging of innocent men was a frequent, if not standard, occurrence. So this sense of perseverance and sanguine attitude that I try to inject in the last stanza is down to knowing that this is just one cruel fate not on the menu for us today. The objective was to try to embed the notion that every setback can be a new beginning, as long as you're not hanging by the neck fighting for your last breath in 18th-century Paddington.[3]

1 V. A. C. Gatrell, *The Hanging Tree: Execution and the English People 1770–1868* (Oxford University Press, 1994)
2 Nigette M. Spikes, *Dictionary of Torture* (Abbott Press, 2015)
3 Frank McLynn, *Crime and Punishment in Eighteenth-century England* (Routledge, 1989)

Russian tour 2014. Poster by Ian Johnsen

RAT RACE

My heart beats in my head and it's thunderous
Those caught in the rat race plunder us
They know what's best for us

Gotta keep up, gotta get ahead
Gotta go and get a job and work 'til I'm dead
And I'm thinking that they must have missed the point
We just hold on for an exit …

Out to deplete, out to defeat everyone
Out to deceit, out to deceive anyone
They're automatically given the authority
Why? I don't know, it's a vile monstrosity

You see the purpose of the rat race defeats me
When we're gone, what's left behind?
But there seems to be no end and no reason
Yet we still carry on

When you finally reach the front of the pack
There's nothing there, just an endless barren track
It goes on and on

You know what?
Let's get disqualified

Christmas show, Liverpool 2014. Poster by Ian Johnsen

RADIATE

To take away our expression is to impoverish our existence

It's insatiable; what we're waiting for

So to keep us from falling apart
We'll write songs in the dark
And to keep us from fading away
We'll write for a better day

It will flourish, it will thrive
It will nourish; a spring cleaning of the mind

They silence and censor our right to create
In cells we choke, without what is innate

This vomiting of anguish, an eruption of the soul
To radiate energy, to comfort and console
To scatter our thoughts, to splatter our spirit
A blizzard of fire, with all we transmit

THE MINI ERA

SWEEP

Sweden, December 2018 – Tom Pullen

THE APPEAL & THE MINDSWEEP I

This is an appeal to the struggling and striving stakeholders of this planet;
This floating rock we call Earth …

Alas, that means you

That means:
Every one of your acquaintance
Every figure your eyes skim past in the street
Every charlatan still to defeat
Every tender face you find solace in

Now mimic the mindset William Wallace was in
Dismount - disembark - descend from your existence
Slacken your *angst* and decant your *hate*
'Cos in the long run *they're about as useful*
As pouring acid onto your dinner plate

To muzzled masses that lead lives of deafening desperation:
With Excalibur aloft King Arthur earned the throne
But it's our minds we got to wrench out of stone

Don't be fooled by its simplicity
There was never a broadcast made of such urgency
'Cos at no time before us
Did we grasp the scope of this emergency

Ladle out love and logic by the boatload
Equipped with that cargo you can take any road
Now grab life; seize time
This fight is for human kind

I am a mindsweeper - focus on me - I will read your mind

I dart through rapids; through streams of thought
Then suddenly I started losing my mind
Catapulting through the uncharted
I could no longer tell if these were your thoughts or mine

It was as if I held a mirror up to my soul
Who was the author?
And who was the observer?
For at the last analysis, our thoughts coalesced

You are not alone

You have entered volatile territory
You have started a journey; you're part of this story
And this, this was just a glimpse

You've no idea what you've got yourself into …

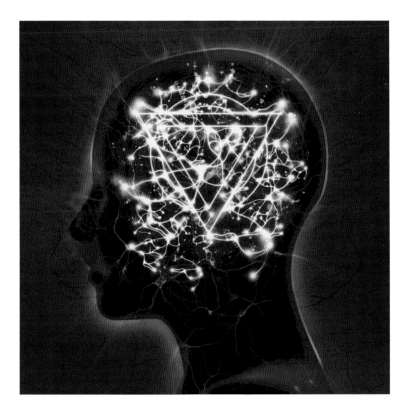

The Mindsweep. Album sleeve by Luke Insect

Berlin show 2016. Poster by Ian Johnsen

Both *Common Dreads* and *A Flash Flood Of Colour* begin with dramatic opening monologues. This album continues that tradition introducing the album's main themes; from encouraging a flexible open-minded outlook in life, to the essentiality of love and logic and the importance of discarding ego and outdated ideas.

Then begins a story – a tale of personal discovery set in a dystopian future. Our protagonist works as a 'mindsweeper'; a fictitious occupation that involves reading people's minds in order to dispel any unwanted or unwarranted ideas. Clearly this is an invasive act by the State in order to keep its populace 'in line' with what they deem to be the acceptable confines of thought. This idea is of course influenced by Orwell's 'thinkpol' or 'thought police' in his classic novel, *1984*.

Our protagonist, halfway through another routine job, finds himself venturing into areas of the brain where memories, emotions, hopes and dreams are all stored. It is here – whilst observing the thoughts and feelings of his patient – that he has an epiphany; these thoughts are almost identical to his own. When reduced to the necessities of survival, as well as to fears and hopes, this human being is no different from himself. This is the grounding for the last line on the album "Mutato nomine, de te fabula narratur".[1]

Our protagonist finds himself panicked by this discovery and becomes lost amongst his patient's thoughts, now indistinguishable from his own. His only comfort in this dangerous biological state is the realisation that neither he, his patient, nor anyone else, is ever truly alone. Behind the wall of our exterior – our appearance and behaviour – we are made of the same stuff. We are united by the same fears, the same needs, the same habitat and the same wider fate. Therefore the despotic nature of his current society now becomes not only incomprehensible but contemptible to him.

'The Mindsweep' is the direct suppression or discrediting of any new ideas by those in power. New ideologies, new technologies, new philosophies – they are all vehemently fought against if they are deemed dangerous to the status quo. Our current system and its guardians have put a leash on human progress to safeguard their way of life. Throughout The Mindsweep I address some of the areas in which new ideas are withheld, I attempt to describe why that is the case and I also try to present some of the plausible resolutions.

[1] Translates from Latin as 'with the name changed the story is told of you'.

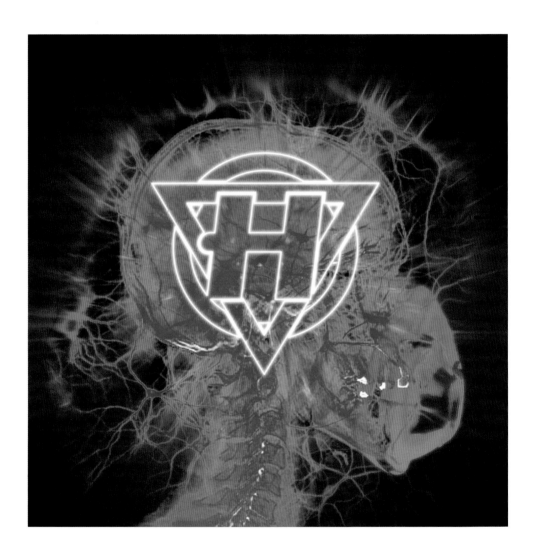

The Mindsweep – Hospitalised. Album sleeve by Luke Insect

THE ONE TRUE COLOUR

As one child is taught red on his mother's knee – the one true colour
A neighbour is taught blue on his mother's knee – the one true colour
With a fervour inherited, it will be subsequently delivered
Ignore the spectrum

Dear whom it may concern,
I feel as though I'm about to crash and burn
I think I'm falling and there's no return
But I've no idea to whom this may concern
I'm looking out at all the stars and I learn
There's no one up above to hear me yearn
I'm on my own

In the arena of the endless unknown
Do not stage theatre and call it truth
And when one child is taught red on his mother's knee
It must be subsequently delivered
With all of the spectrum

Someone has whipped the carpet from beneath my feet
Someone upturned the furniture in my mind
But oh how rich the soil
How wondrous the upheaval
It's time to embark …

To dissect is to broaden the adventure and enrich one's tenure
So do not blunt the surgeon's knife

There's so much to explore; there's so much to absorb
And then the atoms that you borrowed
They are returned to the cosmos
They are returned when you're …

In his 2006 book *The God Delusion*, Richard Dawkins states 'We are all atheists about most of the gods humanity has ever believed in. Some of us just go one god further'. There are an estimated 4,200 different religious groups currently existing on Earth,[1] and that's not even counting different sects; for instance there are 41,000 denominations of Christianity alone.[2] Is there any other phenomenon as divisive as religion?

On every corner of the globe parents are indoctrinating their children into specific faith groups. In effect, they are teaching their children to be close-minded about the nature of the universe and indifferent or even hostile to the wide spectrum of other faiths and ideologies. 'The One True Colour' is a reference to the egotistical and often inflammatory way each religion asserts its own deity as the *only* true deity. The metaphor of visually limiting ourselves to one frequency of light is not a wholly unreasonable comparison, especially when you consider how faith can stunt our perception and outlook.

After talking to many people about losing their religion and having experienced an early epiphany towards atheism myself, the chorus of this piece portrays the discomforting panic that may occur at first – as with a dismantling of any perceived truth – but also the blossoming of enlightenment and fulfilment that follows upon freeing oneself from the chains of doctrine.

If there is one thing that is certain in this life, it's that when someone declares that they know huge truths about the universe without citing proof – and usually reversing the burden of proof by stating that *you* cannot prove *them* wrong – they should be immediately ignored. This is what the first two lines of the second verse attempt to express; you do not know how the universe came to be, you do not know if a higher power is looking after you (whilst simultaneously ignoring the majority of impoverished Africa then?) and you do not know the wishes, whims or indeed the sexual preferences of this higher power! Someone who claims this knowledge with no proof is nothing but a charlatan and will never aid discourse or progress.

The truth is we don't even know what 95% of the universe actually is yet![3] But humanity is trying to understand, it is progressing, it is learning. Science does not claim to have all the answers, but with determination and modesty it perseveres in trying to uncover them. Those, on the other hand, that tell you they do have all the answers – these are the people not to be trusted (especially when their 'proof' sights mediocre books written in the stone age with their core moral content borrowed from earlier philosophers).

The latter half of this track is an ode to knowledge and discovery. It is no secret that much music and art throughout history was written for the glory of the various gods in vogue at the time. Well, this is an attempt at describing the glory of reality and discovery through music. Science is often ridiculed for being 'cold' or 'sterile' in reference to its willingness to demystify or reduce wholes into parts but in the closing paragraphs of this piece I argue that "to dissect is to broaden the adventure". The more we find out, the more fascinating our reality becomes. Remember when we were young and we incessantly (to our parents' irritation) questioned everything? Inquisitiveness is innate; curiosity is intrinsic to who we are. It's one thing we really are good at.

The self-aggrandising and false notions that we have 'souls', or dominion over other animals, or a special relationship with a 'creator' are not the things that make us special. As Stephen Hawking says 'We are just an advanced breed of monkeys on a minor planet of a very average star'. In reality our uniqueness comes from our thirst and our ability to discover and understand. As Hawking continues 'We can understand the Universe. That makes us something very special'.[4] So let us strive to understand more instead of being shepherded or stunted by fear and fiction. For centuries religion has hindered intellectual, philosophical and scientific growth. It is one of the oldest and most prevalent suppressor of new ideas. The original 'Mindsweep'.

Addendum: The lyrics of this piece appear to end prematurely, but the missing word at the end of that last sentence is spelt out by the long chord that the music finishes on. The notes of the chord are D, E, A and D. This then introduces the theme of 'The Last Garrison'; be thankful for the atoms that gave you life, the atoms that you temporarily borrowed from the universe.

1 Adherents.com
2 Center Of Study Of Global Christianity at Gordon-Conwell Theological Seminary (2011)
3 'What is Dark Energy?' (NASA.gov)
4 *Der Spiegel* (17 October, 1988)

Budapest, Hungary. Aug 2016 – Jordan Hughes

ANAESTHETIST

Doctor, fetch the anaesthetist
I want to go under the knife, I believe in this

You fucking spanner
Just a cog in the industrial complex
You shed your blood for the conflicted
You parasite
You're playing god and you don't care who it affects
You suck the blood of the afflicted

Illness is not an indulgence which you should pay for
Nor is it a crime for which you should be punished
For this conviction I would endanger my health

"Shut it, just consume, crave riches and lust for fame"
No you won't see us participating in that game
Keep your twisted take on success
'Cos all I really want is what's beating in your chest

"We drink to your health
But just to inform, this round's on you
And every day you roll the dice
We drink to your health
We capitalise on your condition
Bad luck? You pay the price."

You sold us short
You will not profit off our health

Step the fuck back

When I was 10 years old my parents took me to my first protest march. We were to campaign against the closure of our local hospital. I marched along gallantly, proudly waving my homemade, self-drawn banner aloft. But inside I was blissfully naive and felt nothing more than simple confusion at the prospect of closing a building that 'makes people better'.

Forward to 2015 and after witnessing so many more hospital closures and drastic funding cuts to the UK's National Health Service (NHS), that feeling of young bewilderment had flourished into vehement anger. Now I understood why the slow but relentless gutting of public services had been happening all those years.

Emerging from the devastation of the Second World War in 1948, Britain, after much deliberation, established state funded healthcare. This meant any human regardless of their economic status could receive free medical treatment and it would be funded by national taxes. The health minister at the time, Aneurin Bevan (who I quote in the song), fought long and hard for its construction and stated this beautiful truth: 'no society can legitimately call itself civilised if a sick person is denied medical aid because of lack of means.'[1] This evidently harks back to a time when politicians still had some sense of morality, then.

Russia, New Zealand and most of Scandinavia all implemented universal healthcare around the same time and much of the world has followed suit since then. This song is influenced by two current realities. First of all when touring countries without universal healthcare (namely the U.S.) we've met many people struggling with medical bills who often rely on charity from family, friends and even strangers. Their lives are not only impacted by the cruel misfortune of say, cancer for example, they also have the anxiety of appealing for money to finance the necessary treatments. This is truly heartbreaking. As more jobs vanish due to technological innovation, the unemployed and the poor are the ones who need this safety net more than any of us. The lottery of birth – one's parents, one's genes, one's class – should not ascertain who gets access to health services and who doesn't. Secondly, the current political landscape in Britain is one of privatisation. The Conservative government is slyly selling off large portions of the National Health Service to private companies. This is bad news for two salient reasons. Firstly, it will mean reverting back to paying for one's own treatment, putting the stricken, the unfortunate and the disadvantaged at great risk. And secondly, if a health institution is 'for-profit' then profits come first and patients are put second.[2] Tony Benn, another British politician and somewhat of a hero for Shikari once said 'if we can find the money to kill people, we can find the money to help people'.[3] This really is what it comes down to. I'd rather a healthy society with a well-funded health service offering the best treatment, care and technology, operating at the forefront of medical research.

1 Aneurin Bevan, *In Place of Fear* (Kessinger Publishing, 2010)
2 http://nhap.org/campaigning/join-us-nhs-fightback/nhs-faqs/
3 from an interview in Michael Moore's movie *Sicko* (2007)

Budapest, Hungary. Aug 2016 – Jordan Hughes

THE LAST GARRISON

Can you hear the war cry?
The adrenaline bursts through the riverbanks
Welcome to the #skirmish

"I can't feel my legs!
Give me morphine!
Give me morphine!
Give me more!"

No doubt, this is a tragedy for all
But it ain't over yet
Now heads up and thank fuck you're still alive!

There's still air in my lungs - still blood in my veins
We're part of the last garrison
Still alive

I want to lie here and soak up the sun
But do not alight here, you cannot outrun
"This could be the end" he said, "the end my child"
So I made good use of my face and I smiled

Can you hear the war-cry?
The epinephrine ploughs through the barriers
Welcome to the #skirmish

"I can't feel my arms!
Give me opium!
Give me opium!
Give me hope!"

Let's toast to the fact we got this far …

Life can often seem like a tumultuous onslaught of ups and downs; of good times and bad; the euphoric and the arduous. Our circumstances can change in a flicker of an eyelid. This song represents the relentless fluctuation of the state of affairs in our lives. Sometimes it's beneficial to take a step back from everything and appreciate the honour that it is to simply be alive. We're able to inhale air, to witness the beauty of our planet and to hear the wonders of rhythm and harmony. What a privilege it is to experience so much in such a relatively small pocket of time.

If you're reading this, you are alive today thanks to an inconceivably long and unbroken line of successful acts of procreation that spans back millennia. Pair that with the fact you yourself have cheated death for however many years it is you've been on this planet. What a bloody immense magnitude of luck we've all had just to make it this far. I'll toast to that!

Constellations Festival. Hungary 2016. Poster by Ian Johnsen / photo Tom Pullen

NEVER LET GO OF THE MICROSCOPE

Like Socrates I only graze on the slopes
Of the summit of my own ignorance
Like Hippocrates I can affirm that the method of science
Is an appliance that emancipates us from dogma
And slant
And bias

Ah the seasons are changing …

The velocities at which we now evolve
Mean we've got to dissolve unchecked tradition
But atrocities go untouched under the guise of culture
Committed on another mind another heartbeat
Heartbeat
Heartbeat

I've got a sinking feeling …

Like Sophocles we now wield the paintbrush
So keep a tight grip on a magnifying glass
Our priorities now that we hold the torch
Mean we got to hold it high to illuminate the dark
And archaic
And vile

We swear allegiance to no one

We'll never let go of the microscope
No matter how callous the shells

We'll harness the heat of the sun
And we'll burn you out of fucking existence

This piece builds on the basic philosophy of the original badman himself, Socrates. He famously said 'The unexamined life is not worth living'.[1] The title of this song is an echo of that sentiment. It is becoming increasingly apparent just how important it is for us to analyse our societies, their actions and their values. This piece further develops the line from our 2011 single 'Destabilise': "don't ever respect conventional thought without reason".

It's very easy to enter this world and cower at the might of the various institutions and cultures that structure our lives. We often accept our established customs, behaviours and social constructs as mighty and unalterable. They are part of the fabric of modern life, because these things are so much older and larger and more complicated than ourselves. They are regarded as permanent; a concrete normality.

Another incredible man in Greek history is Hippocrates whose thinking on this subject I attempt to elucidate tersely in verse one. The scientific method – the formulation, testing and moderation of hypothesis – is the greatest tool humanity has, not only for our progress but also for our protection from outdated or detrimental ideas.

Unfortunately we often overlook the ideals of ancient Athenian analysis and find ourselves perpetuating very archaic and irrefutably harmful traditions. One of the more extreme customs that influences the sheer anger in the last stanza of this piece is the atrocity that is female genital mutilation (FGM).[2] Beliefs and practices like these hide behind the protective veil of culture which seemingly allows the act to be 'off grounds' to criticism or prohibitive action. A tolerance for other people's beliefs is commendable, but when other people's beliefs culminate in child abuse we must exchange our reverence for abhorrence and we must put a stop to it.

One should encourage and be enthused by multiculturalism, but to forbid acts like these wouldn't be preventing multiculturalism, it would be preventing barbarism. Moral relativism (the philosophy which posits that what is right and wrong changes depending on what culture or society you are in) is a buried philosophy. When prolonged pain and suffering are the only tangible outcomes of an action, we can then truly label it as objectively or universally negative. Even the usually out of bounds subject of morality becomes accountable to science once you concede that, as the neuroscientist & philosopher Sam Harris says: 'morality is linked to the wellbeing of conscious creatures'.[3]

The great Greek playwright Sophocles is name-dropped next. He is used only as a metaphor to illustrate just how uniquely powerful we now are as a species. We are perfectly capable of magnitudes unthinkable to people living a thousand years ago and, thanks to human insight and advances, a thousand years in the future will be just as unthinkable to us. We have learnt so much as a species and are now so powerful we can write our own future, with humans now not only controlling ecosystems but also the long term direction of our planet's climate. It is clear for the first time in history that *we* are the playwrights writing and directing Earth's future. We are entirely aware of the horrific future we could summon through short-sighted hubris and we are entirely aware of the bright future we *could* summon through aligning ourselves with nature.

This again hammers home the real importance of continual societal analysis.

1 'Apology' by Plato (An account of Socrates' death, from a speech in 399BC)
2 http://en.wikipedia.org/wiki/Female_genital_mutilation
3 Sam Harris, *The Moral Landscape* (Black Swan, 2012)

MYOPIA

Drip drip drop – bit by bit – it's the dulcet sound of the glacial melt
Accompanied by the Beluga, singing about the hand they've been dealt
The Emperor and the Arctic Fox listen intently …

"I'm beginning to get glimpses of what is called real life"
He says, meaning misfortune
"Yes, they're lost in myopia"

Surrounded by ostriches with mouths full of sand
Their teeth grind the grains, but their faces don't contort
Perplexed, I am unable to breathe in their skin

We are all vertebrates but where is their backbone now?

As the Emperor watches his numbers plummet
They hear him scream:
"They're living in denial of science
They're happy to defile silence"

Deprived is the polar bear, grasping at straws
To safeguard dividends they depend on disbelief
Perplexed I am unable to breathe in their skin

I've always loved fables. The only book I got truly invested in during English Literature class in secondary school was George Orwell's *Animal Farm*. This piece is influenced by that classic novel and uses the tactic of anthropomorphism to continue on what has become a central topic for Enter Shikari, climate change and the failure of mankind to act accordingly and responsibly.[1] The characters are all animals from the polar regions and are directly affected by climate change. Throughout the piece they relay their dejection and anger towards the current environmental predicament.

For some time now there has been unequivocal consensus with 97% of scientists agreeing anthropogenic climate change is a reality[2] and a future with the continuation of a 'business as usual' model looks utterly terrifying.[3] Utilising the old adage of ostriches burying their heads in the sand, the 'ostriches' here represent the selfish and short-sighted attitude typically inspired by big business or capitalism in general. The animals, in a state of helpless disbelief, ask "we are all vertebrates, but where is their backbone now?". This frustrated plea to humanity hopes to strike a surge of empathy in us all. The unifying description of themselves and humans as 'vertebrates' is intended to remind us of the glorious fact that every animal on this planet is related to one another. We are all evolutionary cousins, however distant. If you go back far enough on your family tree (far beyond the usual few generations) you discover that you even share an ancestor with a fish! We're bound together by our evolutionary history and by the fact that we share a common home – this floating sphere of rock. But unfortunately, instead of acting in solidarity with our evolutionary cousins in the face of this existential threat, we have allowed the corporate whims of short-term profit and relative stability to consolidate a position of stubborn stagnancy.

We do have plenty of 'backbone'; we have the determination, ingenuity and technological knowhow to address climate change. In fact the problem of climate change doesn't even really exist, there is only really a problem of ignorance. The energy institutions cling on to the current infrastructure to ensure profit 'safety' and downplay all the new possibilities. Therefore, 'Mindsweep' becomes rife.

1 A topic addressed during every era of the band from 'Mothership' to 'No Sleep Tonight' to 'Arguing With Thermometers'
2 'Consensus: 97% Of Climate Scientists Agree' (NASA.gov)
3 Mark Lynas, *Six Degrees: Our Future on a Hotter Planet* (Harper Perennial, 2008)

Tokyo, Japan. Dec 2014 – Tom Martin

TORN APART

A naked eye
Conspires with fear
To form an idea
So destructive and insincere

Reared in the mind
But outside you'll find
That nature does not align

You see,
There's more variation within populations than between populations

Ah for too many years
A myth perseveres
The scars and the souvenirs

Defined by your skin
Forget we share kin
We're torn apart

It feels as though we're sinking
I don't know how we'll get to shore again
Sinking, we'll surface through the waves

Look back to the past
We hail from one caste
This division will not last

Our species, 'Homo Sapiens' (which means 'wise man' in Latin) constructed the concept of hierarchical 'race' in the 18th century.[1] Back then, they actually divided up humanity into a hierarchy, with whites (or Caucasians) at the top and Africans at the bottom. No prizes for guessing who came up with that ranking system, then … White biologists. This pervasive idea then went on to generate such horrific acts as apartheid, genocide, holocaust and slavery. 'Wise man' indeed!

With this piece I concentrated on the simple fact that biologically and genetically speaking, the concept of race is actually a contentious subject and may not even exist to any great useful degree. We immediately experience problems as soon as we think in categorical terms when it comes to describing humanity. For instance, Caucasians and Africans are not two separate peoples; to say that is to ignore their shared heritage. Our species' history is concise; the ancestors of everyone alive on Earth populated the world after descending from Africa.

With only the 'naked eye', fear and (in hindsight) ignorance as one's tools, it's easy to see how the 'destructive idea' of race was created. And we are still suffering from the hangover of this early notion today, with the idiocy that is 'racism'.

Through a series of genetic discoveries made during the 70's it was found that 75–85% of genetic variability in humans is found *within* perceived 'races' and not *between* 'races'.[2] That is to say, the bulk of biological differences between humans are actually between one person and another, rather than from one race (or population) to another. One study puts it like this; 'The considerable genetic differences we see between individuals has very little to do with so-called "racial" boundaries. Rather, it is merely the variation that was present in the original human population that seeded all the current human populations.'[3] Since this finding many have argued that the social construct of 'race' itself is therefore virtually useless.[4] If just 6–10% of genetic differences correlate to 'racial' or "continental human groups",[5] why do we use that as the definitive way to group humans? If 75–85% of genetic differences are between individuals, is it not reasonable to deduce that we are all in fact just individuals? And we belong to one race; the human race?

The visual basis for race (the external differences, or simply, how we look) may disappear completely in the future[6] rendering the concept of race as we have it today, a petty temporary notion soon to become outdated. Every individual needs to be free to construct their own identity without having various categories imposed on them, whether race-based or class-based as 'There's A Price On Your Head' explores. The fact that we are all related isn't just a naively romantic or 'cute' subjective idea but is one backed by biology – society just hasn't caught up yet.

1 It is important to note that the division of humanity into a hierarchy of races was not a feature of ancient Rome or ancient Greece. Historical records show us that their societies had both black and white citizens and they did not equate differences in skin pigmentation with human worth. Oh, for sure they had slaves but they were usually captives of war regardless of skin colour.

2 Richard Lewontin, *The Apportionment of Human Diversity* (1972)

3 Yi-Fan Lu, David B. Goldstein et al. *Personalized Medicine And Human Genetic Diversity* (July, 2014)

4 *Human Genetic Variation* (Wikipedia)

5 Alan R Templeton, *Human Races in the Context of Recent Human Evolution* (2003)

6 *Projecting Human Evolution: 5 Traits We Might Possess In The Future*, Mother Nature Network, (May, 2012)

Wrexham, UK. Feb 2016 – Alexey Makhov

THE BANK OF ENGLAND

I refuse to notice the wind or the rain
To teach me of nature would be done in vain
I ignore all - I just contain

Predicated on a great disconnect
I don't react and I do not reflect
I ignore all - I just retain

The invisible hand no longer guides, it chokes

They blew up the Bank of England
The paper burnt for days

In the end we all employ sabotage
No room for ethics now, greed is in charge
I ignore all - I just constrain

How many barrels are left in the field?
I only care for the coins that you yield
I ignore all - I just obtain

We have entered an era where you no longer have to be Karl Marx or some other prestigious economist or philosopher to observe and understand the flaws of capitalism. This piece mainly focuses on a notable contribution to the philosophy of Capitalism from Adam Smith (a man often said to be the father of modern economics). Smith is well-known for a concept he calls the 'invisible hand': 'Every individual neither intends to promote the public interest, nor knows how much he is promoting it … He intends only his own gain, and he is in this, as in many other cases, led by an invisible hand … By pursuing his own interest he frequently promotes that of the society more effectually than when he really intends to promote it.'[1] What Adam Smith is postulating here is that even though the way we act within a capitalist system is selfish in intention, it will actually serve a positive social outcome in the long run. This may have been the case in Smith's time but today with 1% of people owning half of the world's wealth[2] and with one billion people starving,[3] it is clear that this is not a world where public interest has been 'effectually promoted'. The 'invisible hand' implies the benefit of everyone but in reality benefits only a small subsection of the population.

The line "in the end we all employ sabotage" is a reference to a quote by Thorstein Veblen, a prominent 20th century economist: 'All business sagacity reduces itself in the last analysis to judicious use of sabotage'.[4] This beautiful but hefty word salad basically means that to succeed in business you must frequently sabotage others. Concisely put; it's a dog-eat-dog world out there yo!

As time goes on, the defence of capitalism becomes less and less watertight. Diminishing resources and climate change are just two of the phenomena of which Smith's era had no grasp. These two matters could not have been foreseen but now force the whole ideology of market economics into disarray. We cannot keep consuming infinitely on a finite planet and we cannot keep burning fossil fuels – an act that will destroy life as we know it. With the exponential rise of technological capability, a world has been formulated that could, and must, put that final nail in the coffin of capitalism.

Even though this archaic system ignores the very realities of nature, we still strangely cling on to it, mainly due to the 'Mindsweep' employed by the custodians of the status quo. We disconnect ourselves from the damage it has done and the dangerous path it is leading humanity down. The stark but obviously figurative image of a burning bank is the ominous warning of what to expect if a radical shift in how we structure our world is not implemented. To quote Martin Luther King 'a riot is the language of the unheard'.[5]

Many hold something akin to religious fervour when it comes to protecting market economics and without any real consideration of alternatives, continue to employ 'Mindsweep' to silence economic dissenters or pioneers. We must continue to publicise capitalism's causal disposition when it comes to modern predicaments. And let us hope we can update our way of life before our situation goes from drastic to helpless.

1 Adam Smith, *The Wealth of Nations vol. IV* (Penguin, 1776)
2 The World Food Programme, *Number Of World's Hungry Tops A Billion* (June 2009)
3 'Working For The Few' (Oxfam, 2014)
4 Thorstein Veblen, *An Inquiry Into the Nature of Peace, and the Terms of Its Perpetuation* (The Macmillan Company, 1917)
5 Martin Luther King, Jr., *The Other America* (March 1968)

Cardiff, UK. Feb 2016 – Alexey Makho

THERE'S A PRICE ON YOUR HEAD

I am upper class
Upper middle lower class

I am lower class
Lower upper middle class

I am upper middle class; **I am living in the past**

Yeh, there's a price on your head, unknown to you
There's a fucking price on your head

I am lower class
Upper middle lower class

I am upper class
Lower upper middle class

I am lower class
Upper middle lower class

I am upper lower class; **I am living in the past**

"But we must have structure Mr Reynolds"

Born scarred?

Let us heal

There's a famous behavioural experiment performed on Capuchin monkeys (as well as other primates and mammals) that plays out as follows:

Two monkeys are given rewards in the form of chunks of cucumber every time they perform a simple task. After a few repetitions of the task, one monkey is given a more nutritious and tasty reward in the form of a grape. The other witnesses this and excitedly performs the simple task again, only now with raised expectations. But he still receives a cucumber … he reacts with anger and throws the chunk back at the human experimenter in indignation![1]

A sense of fairness is not just an important concept in human behaviour.

Another characteristic we share with our primate cousins is the employment of social hierarchies. We structure our populations into 'classes', with the leaders and the followers, the powerful and the dependant, the rich and the poor. Straightaway this seems like two contradicting ideas. On the one hand we have natural tendencies towards a sense of fairness, justice and equality. We even have an innate drive to help each other when there is no reward or chance of reciprocity. Altruism and the ability of making others happy simply makes us happy. This is juxtaposed though with the way we structure our citizenry unequally through social ranks. Today society is still reminiscent of a feudal pyramid hierarchy, with the wealthy few at the top and the struggling many at the bottom.[2]

This piece's lyrical basis is influenced by George Orwell's views on class structure in society. He often sardonically labelled his background as "lower–upper middle class".[3] We are all born into families we didn't chose, into societies we didn't chose and we are certainly not born equal. We are separated and branded from day one, fed supposed realities about our worth and our relevance. We often hear of 'rags to riches' stories where a working class person fights their way to the top through talent and hard work. This, of course, is not a reasonable account of actuality and more a reflection of the media's grasp of sensationalism than of widespread occurrence. Most of those born poor will stay poor. And those born rich will have to be incredibly foolish not to remain rich. There is a real sense of self-worth aligned with these labels and this does nothing but increase the psychological divide between these artificial groups.

There is now a colossal body of evidence to prove that inequality is socially corrosive. The book *The Spirit Level: Why Equality Is Better For Everyone*[4] manages to collate the undeniable statistics and present them clearly. Most immediate and striking are the visual formats where we can easily observe that more unequal societies do worse according to almost every quality of life indicator, from physical and mental health, to violence and imprisonment, from education and trust between strangers, to obesity and child well-being.

Even the richest (no matter whether they agree or not) are better off in more equal societies. But the gap keeps getting bigger; the richest 1% of humans own 46% of the world's wealth. And seven out of ten people live in countries where economic inequality has increased in the last 30 years.[5] As a frightening and testing future lies ahead, now is the time that humanity needs to be working together more than ever and ridding our societies of the archaic and stultifying structures of such rigid wealth disparity.

1 'Monkeys Reject Unequal Pay' a study by Frans de Waal & Sarah Brosnan
   (Emory University, 2003)
2 This was what the *A Flash Flood Of Colour* artwork was attempting to represent, a complete
   overhaul of the pyramid societal structure; turning the triangle upside down.
3 George Orwell, *The Road To Wigan Pier* by (Penguin Modern Classics, 1937)
4 R. Wilkinson & K. Pickett, *The Spirit Level: Why Equality Is Better For Everyone*
   (Penguin Books, 2010)
5 'Working For The Few' (Oxfam, 2014)

DEAR FUTURE HISTORIANS

I never walked on the moon
I never saw the pyramids
I was never struck by famine or fortune
I'll never experience the world you inhabit
I never swam with dolphins
I never sang from a mountain top
I was no inventor and no archaeologist

I fret not, for I made my own discovery

Just put your weight on my shoulders

For when I dive into your iris
My brain erupts into biochemical mayhem
And I feel like a man with two hearts

Love, without doubt, is one of the most ubiquitous topics artists, philosophers, poets and composers have endeavoured to depict or describe for centuries. But unfortunately, today, modern pop music has done us the disservice of saturating the subject into a cliché-filled, cringe-inducing, anodyne area of artistic expression.

This piece starts with a list of life-affirming, awe-inspiring experiences that I place subordinate to the comfort and strength of a loving relationship. This is because love often feels so encapsulating that everything else can pale into insignificance. Addressed to future historians, this list will probably seem rather quaint to those living in the future (if we imagine an optimistic view of the future, of course). It is not too hard to envisage a world where space travel, trips to world heritage sights and having a quality of life far better than we have now is taken for granted; somewhat of a banality! This, I hope, bolsters the claim that however unremarkable my list of comparisons are or however unimaginable future lists of comparisons would be, love, compassion, adoration, kindness; these are still the most important and valuable faculties of our species.

With this piece I wanted to reclaim the concept of love as something still worth approaching through alternative art forms. I decided to concentrate on the biological aspects of love for my inspiration. For instance, when we are in love the threshold for experiencing positive emotions is lowered substantially, therefore the pleasure centres in our brain are activated far more easily. We begin to construct a romanticised view of the world around us. Happiness is attained more easily and the pain and aversion centres in our brain begin to fire less frequently. Continuing with the recurring use of anatomical language on this album, I try to communicate this reality with the line "I feel like a man with two hearts".

We also experience what Jacque Fresco terms 'extensionality'.[1] The willingness to support, assist and extend the possibilities of another; to take on another's struggles. So the simplicity of John Lennon's message of 'All you need is love' and his concentration and activism around the ideal appears to have real empirical importance as well. Compassionate love has the power to make us far more amicable and empathic. This piece is an open letter to the historians of the future – a small bit of humble advice from the past, do not forge a world where love isn't absolutely central and salient.

1   Jacque Fresco, *The Best That Money Can't Buy: Beyond Politics, Poverty & War* (2002)

London, UK. Feb 2016 – Alexey Makhov

THE APPEAL & THE MINDSWEEP II

I am a mindsweeper - focus on me - I will read your mind

It goes on and on through volatile territory
Through the plains of adversity and the ravines of neurosis
Through the veins of gods and the valley of death

But remember you are not alone

And we dance like knights

Here come the cavalry
The same blood gushes through my veins
Feel it surge
Sweep through jet streams
Down axons
And across synapses

Mutato nomine, de te fabula narratur

Hasselt, Belgium, Aug 2015 – Jordan Hughes

Slipshod video illustration & animation by Peter MacAdams

SLIPSHOD

"Oi fucks, let's eat 'ere, it looks nice"

Get me the manager!
"Oh dear, what seems to be the problem sir?"

- First of all,
I was greeted with a grimace
Service with a sneer
He don't want to be here

- Second of all,
I was seated by the window
And the draft was a serious inconvenience

- There was lipstick on my glass and it wasn't mine

- We put our order in - I can't believe the time

- This is a shambles, your cook is a heathen

- Your carpet is ugly and your veg ain't in season

My impatience spread like gravy on a tablecloth
And your head looks like it was carved out of a nut
Rory C, tell 'em …
I was waiting in line for 10 whole minutes
This is unacceptable - you're pushing me to my limits!

"Please don't raise your voice in here sir
This is a respected establishment
I'm sure we can sort this out quietly, no?"

Oh really? Well that's a great vase you got there
It'd be a real shame if something happened to it …

Slipshod, kick it

Redshift. Single sleeve by Ian Johnsen / black hole image by Mike Tyler

REDSHIFT

We drift apart …

If there's one reason to smile, it's when you look up out at night
You're fortunate enough to drink in a vista
A hundred billion flares display a glowing history
Splayed out across a canvas, the night sky

But for a moment just contemplate
When looking up, you only saw a blank slate
And for a moment just contemplate
It appears that heaven's been abandoned

We accelerate through the estate of outer space
We separate, we fragment

I climb down from the wall
Where I sit and search for a source of light
Other than our dear sun, the lone star

Just contemplate, what if the heavens were abandoned?

Your skin and bones, heart and mind
Are made from the remnants of stars, that died
Can you feel it inside?

A supergiant erupts, into a supernova
The ultimate sacrifice and **we are the descendants**

Edwin Hubble discovered in 1929 that the universe was expanding. He also discovered the further a galaxy is from us, the redder the light waves it emits. This is called 'redshift'. I'm not qualified to go into that any further here, I'll leave that to your physics teacher, but I do have the necessary qualifications to explain the thinking behind the song …

'Redshift' philosophises over two huge findings of 20th century cosmology and my wish was that its lasting emotional effect would be similar to that which 'The Last Garrison' attempts to elicit – gratitude at being alive and an appreciation of the luck involved in your circumstances.

First, we look at the big picture – and I mean the *biggest* of pictures – the age of our universe. I observe how lucky our species is to be alive at this point in the universe's lifespan. We have evolved at the fortunate point where we are able to observe the billions of other galaxies out there and therefore hope to discover other life forms. This isn't just down to our scientific ability but also down to the fact other galaxies are close enough that we are *able* to observe them.

I say this because in a few trillion years from now, any species that develops a scientific civilisation with the ability to look outwards will see a very different picture: a vast, unending empty space. This is because our universe is expanding. But not only is it expanding, it is *accelerating* in its expansion. (If you drew two dots onto a balloon – the dots representing galaxies, and the balloon representing the universe – and then inflated it, you would see the two dots stretch away from each other as the balloon inflates. This is effectively what is happening to every galaxy in our universe.) Galaxies will accelerate outwards and away from each other, eventually reaching the speed of light. At which point, they will become invisible to any observer.

Life forms flourishing at this later point in the universe's existence will come to the conclusion – with all available scientific rigour – that they are alone in a cold and dark universe. A far more lonely and gloomy perspective to have to endure than our current one, right?

The second cosmological aspect of the song appears in the last few stanzas, concentrating on the poetic sentiment "we are all made of stardust". However clichéd, overly romantic or 'emo' this sounds to you, it really is true!

Not all the elements were made during the Big Bang. Carbon, nitrogen, oxygen and iron (some of the elements that we, and all we see, are made from) can only be made in the fiery cores of stars, or more specifically, supernovae. A supernova is, in effect, a 'dying' star. Stars eventually explode, spewing their nutritious 'guts' out into the cosmos in the process. It is these 'starguts' (far more *punk* in its tone than '*star dust*', right?) that contain the vital elements which make up you and me. We are ALL descendants of stars.

A huge shout out goes to Carl Sagan, Neil deGrasse Tyson and Lawrence M. Krauss, not only for being a huge inspiration for these lyrics, and to me in general, but also for their tireless work in science and its popularisation.

Budapest, Hungary. Aug 2015 – Jordan Hughes

HOODWINKER

"This is the voice of God
You got it?
Stay in and lock your doors"

I don't care what you've achieved
There's only one location if you don't follow me
(You always get what you wanted   )
You're gonna burn in a blistering furnace
For now until forever no matter how earnest
(You always get what you wanted …)

Halt, freeze, who goes there?
Do you have the right documentation?

Stop, wait, this ain't right
This is fraudulent, this is counterfeit
You are a hoodwinker, sir

"This is the voice of god; the shrink-wrapper of minds"

I don't care if you're devout
To the three thousand other gods
In every age the priest has been hostile to liberty
Burning books is mental captivity

It's a swindle for your soul

Even now, as fully grown humanoids, we at Enter Shikari have never been able to completely shake off our juvenile sense of humour. Often people expect those who want to change the world to be staunchly pensive people, dedicated to the sombre and serious; exempt from the playful, comic or ironic. This has always vexed us and that's why songs like 'The Feast', 'The Jester', 'Slipshod' and 'Hoodwinker' exist. For me, a sprinkling of facetiousness and parody go hand-in-hand with the criticism of the status quo. Plus, of course, it keeps one from descending into despair when addressing such gloomy subjects!

'Hoodwinker' has one of the most ridiculous openings of any of Enter Shikari track. One of the heaviest riffs we've ever played, providing accompaniment to the crazed, guttural voice of a maniac as he exclaims himself to be "the voice of God", brutishly ordering you to "stay in and lock your doors".

Even in today's world, with its growing atheistic composition and psyche, God is still conjured up to be this benevolent, compassionate being. (I'll attempt to hold back my urge to digress here into my aversion to this misrepresentation. I'll simply ask you, dear reader, to make what you will of a constant pathological demand for worship coupled with an apparent disinterest in widespread famine, disease and death).

Instead of going full-on, fervent, atheist warrior (and let's face it, the world has enough of these) for 'Hoodwinker', I thought I'd instead introduce a kind of quaint British silliness to the subject. Firstly by having God represented by a grievous, bellowing madman and secondly, by having a sort of early-20th century establishment figure question God's documentation, hence the legitimacy of his identity and deity status.

At a time where every political discussion is lead by embittered talk of immigration, and where sadly we see more and more people becoming refugees from homelands that have become war zones (or – looking towards a potential future – of climate change causing yet further displacement and emigration), I thought using the very terrestrial concept of identity, immigration and legitimacy with a proposed 'higher being' would perhaps highlight the nonsensical and monstrous nature of using these concepts with humans.

Brixton, London, UK. January 2019 — Tom Pullen

THE

SPARK

ERA

As body of work, The Spark marked the beginning of a new writing style for me; one focused on revealing my inner experience. While I pride myself on writing music that is first and foremost honest, it has more often than not been outward looking in its commentary. With The Spark, after experiencing a period of rich emotional turmoil, I decided to turn my gaze inward and broadcast my self; my struggles and vulnerabilities. This decision was influenced by a few different factors that I will get to in a minute, below.

Firstly, I wanted to just quickly address the criticism that's been levelled of me supposedly abandoning my earlier, more politically-charged lyrical approach. I would counter that by saying; really, I feel that this is an *equally* politically charged body of work, it just focusses on one of the psychological causes for our current political imbroglio (something that is often overlooked in our patchwork or 'quick fix', profit led, political discourse) instead of lyrics of broad and varied political content. I wanted to delve inside and concentrate on psychology and how it effects larger world outcomes. I wanted to steer completely clear of surface evaluations, sloganeering and political war cries, which is, to some degree, probably what many expected, given the nature of the world at the time of writing *The Spark*; a body of work led by anger and finger-pointing. My contrarian instinct ultimately drove me away from such a response (the world's tumultuous political affairs had also given rise to a rush of knee-jerk and ultimately banal, politically driven pop music, which also urged me further away from this style).

I think now is the time for a subtler, deeper and more nuanced look at the root causes of societal ills, and I attempt to do this by centring this album on human vulnerability and how that should unite us, instead of scaring us into division.

Vulnerability is the default state of our species. Whether you feel a testosterone-fuelled, defensive pang reading this sentence or not, it is simply true. We are fragile creatures. While giraffes are up and running within an hour of being born; while baby sea turtles hatch on the sand and miraculously make their way on their own to the ocean; while most reptiles abandon their eggs before they've even hatched; humans can't even sit unaided for the first six months of their lives. Sure, the new-borns of other primate species rely on caregivers too, but humans are especially helpless because at birth, our brains are comparatively underdeveloped. And that's OK, experts say. Our fragility is the evolutionary trade-off for having highly-developed brains eventually capable of managing complex reasoning and social interaction.

But even after we develop all that computing power, the fragility of our early years never truly leaves us. The human imagination is our biggest source of achievement but also one of our greatest sources of pain; because our wonderful creativity can lead us into being inventive in self-defeating ways, too. Our powerful minds bring with them immense vulnerability. We have inclinations towards over-analysis, and we must endure feelings of doubt, inferiority, anxiety, envy, superstition, unrelenting ambition, hatred, greed and jealousy, and that's just for starters.

Perhaps our adrenal glands and frontal cortex are not tuned for today's stress and strife? They evolved in the plains of Africa after all, where a speedy fight-or-flight response to avoid being eaten by lions was our nervous system's main job! We now find ourselves in a far safer, more technologically and cognitively superior world, but with antiquated biology.

For much of modern Western human history, it has been deemed reasonable to attempt to mask or conceal our susceptibilities. No era more so than in 19th Century England, where showing self-restraint in expressing emotion was paramount. One was expected to 'bottle it up' and keep a 'stiff upper lip' in times of adversity or emotional difficulty. This trait became synonymous with the English. In particular, those who had the misfortune of being brought up in the single-sex public boarding schools, where displaying vulnerable emotions was perceived as a weakness and discouraged, or even punished. Not addressing emotions can result in humans developing low emotional intelligence and can increase the likelihood of destructive behaviour.

(I cannot write this book in 2018 and not mention Donald Trump, so let me get this mention of him out of the way now, and then I can make a solemn promise, dear reader, that you will not encounter his name throughout the rest of these pages). Donald Trump is a man who was sent to private military boarding school, and like many of his generation he will have been told his whole life that for men, emotions are a sign of weakness (excluding anger of course, anger is always acceptable from a male...). The man is 50% pride / 50% fury, encased in the thinnest of skins; a truly awful cocktail. Whenever a question arises that may prick his self-esteem - be it the size of his hands, the poor state of his intellect, or his plethora of failed businesses - his vanity and hubris give him the ability to perform immense mental gymnastics to dismiss the facts and he invariably reacts with instant petty slander towards the disputer.

My vision is of the polar-opposite mindset and of a contrasting society. One inspired by the radical honesty of Rousseau, Montaigne and Schopenhauer (three men who inspired the lyrical content of this album more than anyone). A society where, with ease and composure, we can address our weaknesses and shortcomings, admit our mistakes and mishaps without shame or ridicule, discuss our difficult inner experiences with all our crazy and often dark idiosyncrasies brazenly aired.

We simply must be allowed to be human. And humanity's defining characteristic may well be vulnerability, but it is coupled by an immense ability to examine, probe, analyse, design, create and persevere. So, let us not hide from being bold and being open with ourselves and let us be tolerant, imaginative and understanding with others.

Rou

THE SIGHTS

Are you staying awake for the lift off, tonight?
You'll never believe the sights tonight, the sights tonight, the sights

Mr Magpie,
You got distracted by the gleam the diamonds, as you flew by
But their dull glint does not impress
When there's a billion stars in the sky

I sit, gripping my pen like a bread knife, as I write:
"I'm leaving this earth for the stars tonight"
Now I'm running to board the flight

Now I boldly go into the great unknown
And like Jean-Jacques Rousseau
I give you my mind to be blown
Now I boldly go into the great unknown
Like Marcus Cicero
"While there's life, there's hope"

I'm searching far and wide, to find a planet to orbit
Far and wide, I wanna scan and explore it
Far and wide, you're my new planet to orbit
So fire up the rockets

It's over now
And I'm a little bit petrified of what's to come
Yeh my head's a bit stir fried

It's over now
And I'm a little unqualified
But fire up the rockets

'The Sights' is about a renewed zest for life; the hopeful vista that emerges from a period of adversity. It's about new beginnings and the spectrum of emotions that accompany them, from excitement to anxiety.

The lyric opens with a masochistic in-joke. I remember questioning, during an extreme bout of insomnia, whether I would ever associate difficulty sleeping with a positive emotion again. For instance, we all surely remember not being able to sleep as a child due to some kind of excitement – Christmas, birthdays, the eve of a holiday. I suppose the somewhat cruel realisation is just how similar anxiety and excitement are biologically. The body states in the grasp of these emotions are so similar, that one technique for dealing with anxiety is imagining and acting excited in an attempt to 'hack' or 'fool' your biology. Emerging from a prolonged period of crippling sleeplessness, I thought a bit of dark humour about the situation was apt; I'm asking myself whether I'm staying awake for something exciting, knowing full well that, in fact, the opposite is true.

Using a magpie as my metaphorical scapegoat (a bird that is attracted to shiny things, according to the old wives' tale), I'm making a point about how so often we get attracted to, and even infatuated with, that which is cosmetic and striking, close and attainable, garish and meretricious. We lose sight of the bigger picture and (the usually more helpful) broader analysis. Personally, I spent a good while clinging to various things in my life because they were comforting. I didn't realise (or possibly chose not to realise) how these comforts were actually destructive. Coming to terms with change is a scary business and, looking back, I find it remarkable just how resistant I was. For example, when a long-term relationship is finished, you know a dramatic lifestyle remoulding is about to come. In not thinking with perspective and cool rationality, I clung to the diamonds (the earthly normality) and forgot the stars (the broader picture). But more about that later.

"Now I boldly go, into the great unknown" is the grit and determination I felt after eventually coming to the realisation that I would have to leave behind the comforts of the last few years and embrace change.

In the bridge I namedrop two philosophers, Rousseau and Cicero, whose ideas helped me forge the themes of honest communication and hope from which this album grew. Rousseau's *Confessions*, first published in 1782, was one of the first ever autobiographies, and one in which an individual wrote of his own experiences and personal feelings (the only predecessors to this were the books of religious figures, like Augustine's own *Confessions*, written between AD 397–400). It was, essentially, a psychological self-examination a whole century before psychoanalysis. Rousseau 'justified' this new style of literature beautifully, with the explanation: "I have conceived of a new genre of service to render to man: to offer them the faithful image of one amongst them, in order for them to learn to know themselves." Honestly relaying your inner experiences can help others to make sense of their own.

For me, this became evident whilst talking online about my encounters with generalised anxiety disorder, social anxiety, insomnia, OCD and depression. I saw that I could connect with and help others who had gone through similar experiences and that, equally, I too was aided by their sharing. This was a wonderful, reifying and liberating epiphany – something that of course is self-evident in its basis but, when experienced, is truly appreciated. The somewhat self-absorbed but ultimately important task of revealing what life is like behind one's eyes is what I describe with the line, "I give you my mind to be blown". Offer yourself and your true experience and you will be taken aback and elated by the deep connections it can create with other people.

Also used in the bridge is a proverb that has its origins in a line from one of my favourite Romans, Marcus Cicero: "Aegroto dum anima est, spes esse dicitur" (It is said that for a sick man, there is hope as long as there is life)[1]. This introduces the themes of hope, determination and positivity that fuels the chorus.

In the chorus I allude to the simple universal dream of falling in love again, of finding another planet to orbit. In the more sombre last verse,
I list my negative emotions; fear, disorientation and a feeling of inferiority at the coming changes. Expressing these emotions is a difficult thing for anyone, but especially for men brought up in a society that is still quite adamant that boys should not show vulnerability or emotions perceived as 'weak'.

1 Marcus Tullius Cicero (106 BC – 43 BC), *Epistulae ad Atticum (Letters to Atticus)*, Book IX, Letter X, section 3

enter:shikari

Stop The Clocks Tour. 2019

UK : Jan 2019.
10.01 Sheffield, UK
11.01 Nottingham, UK
12.01 London, UK
13.01 Leicester, UK
15.01 Llandudno, UK
16.01 Liverpool, UK
18.01 Bristol, UK
19.01 Southend, UK
20.01 Norwich, UK
23.01 Glasgow, UK
24.01 Aberdeen, UK
25.01 Inverness, UK
26.01 Preston, UK
28.01 Northampton, UK
29.01 Southampton, UK
30.01 Cambridge, UK

UK : Feb 2019.
01.02 Birmingham, UK
02.02 Leeds, UK
03.02 Manchester, UK
04.02 Newcastle, UK
13.02 London, UK

UA / BY : Mar 2019.
01.03 Lviv, UA
02.03 Kiev, UA
03.03 Kharkiv, UA
05.03 Minsk, BY

RU : Mar 2019.
Moscow, RU 07.03
St Petersburg, RU 09.03
Nizhniy Novgorod, RU 11.03
Krasnodar, RU 13.03
Ekaterinburg, RU 15.03
Rostov-na-Donu, RU 16.03
Krasnoyarsk, RU 18.03
Irkutsk, RU 20.03

EU : Mar 2019.
Lille, FR 27.03
Tilburg, NL 28.03
Strasbourg, FR 29.03
Paris, FR 30.03

EU : Apr 2019.
Milan, IT 01.04
Munich, DE 02.04
Linz, AT 03.04
Budapest, HU 04.04
Prague, CZ 06.04
Dresden, DE 07.04
Berlin, DE 08.04
Leipzig, DE 09.04
Erlangen, DE 11.04
Dortmund, DE 12.04
Cologne, DE 13.04
Wiesbaden, DE 15.04
Saarbrucken, DE 16.04
Brussels, BE 17.04

ENTERSHIKARI.COM

An Ambush Reality & 30 Century Management presentation. In cooperation with Xray Touring.

Berlin, Germany. November 2017 – Tom Pullen

LIVE OUTSIDE

I wanna live outside, live outside of all of this

I keep calling, keep hauling, keep calling them back
I can't stand, can't stand, can't stand this attack
This neuron buzz is on another level
I'm on thin ice, I'm dancing with the devil

I can't sleep with the noise in this house
But you can't beat the allure of this now
I can't sleep with the noise in this house
Why won't they pipe down?

I keep taming, keep training, keep taming the horse
But it's wild, it's feral and it's running its course
Patiently, madness waits in line
In the reception room of my mind

Waiting for the door to be left
Unattended and open for an unwanted guest
And it's so busy I'd be surprised if I even noticed

No they don't even know about us…

Do you ever feel so clouded by your thoughts, so besieged by your fears, so fatigued by the relentless nature of anxiety, that you wish you (your consciousness; your essence) could climb out of your skull and take a break from it all? Perhaps you could perch nonchalantly on your earlobe, just out of earshot of the intensity of your own mind, and finally relax. This track is a rumination on this feeling of longing to escape. Written at the height of my three-month episode of insomnia and the anxiety and OCD that accompanied it, these lyrics are essentially a string of metaphors. Wanting to retreat from the frontline; dancing with evil personified; being unable to sleep in a noisy house; attempting to tame a wild horse; these all felt like valid scenarios with which to compare my inner experience. Constantly trying to battle rumination with logic, or the calm analysis of CBT (Cognitive Behavioural Therapy), or whatever other tools you have at your disposal, can put you constantly on your guard. And madness feels like a very real possibility, biding its time, waiting for that one moment when your mind's door is left unprotected.

Whilst this inner experience rages on, it can often go completely undetected by other people; one's behaviour doesn't always represent one's inner circumstances. This is what is meant by the line "they don't even know about us" – 'us' being myself and the devil I'm dancing with; the horse I'm trying to tame. People can be oblivious to your inner turmoil and that's why it's important for all of us to broadcast our experience, to continue the fight towards the realisation that we are actually similarly vulnerable, and therefore similar, in a world that is becoming increasingly divisive.

Sparky. Birmingham, UK. November 2017 – Tom Pullen

TAKE MY COUNTRY BACK

I don't want to take my country back
I want to take my country forward

But everyone's preaching to their choirs
Words billow up and get trapped in church spires
Wisps of fury against one's neighbour
Reeling around in the echo chamber

Now look what we've done to ourselves
We've really gone and fucked it this time
Look what we've done to ourselves

So get up, get up and feel the rising tide
We're fed up, fed up with all the cyanide

There's anger stashed in the creases of your face
That burning rage could gut a castle
But you torch your neighbour
And now your whole town is ablaze

"Everyone is seeing red"
Laugh the pyromaniacs in the stronghold
Sparking fury against one's neighbour
Twisting the truth with a blamethrower

I feel like we're living on the edge
And the cliff's eroding

If we feel no sense of belonging to the society we inhabit, we will find that sense of belonging in ideology. We will search for answers, for structure, for hope, for identity, for community. With disenchantment as a driver, people can become intimately connected to an idea and, increasingly, ignore critical thought, analysis or other ideas.

"Wisps of fury against one's neighbour"

In recent years, the inequality of the prevailing world order – whether you call it 'neoliberalism', 'globalisation', 'free-market capitalism', or 'business-as-usual politics' – has triggered an angry backlash, as faith in that world order and its ideology has faltered dramatically. Unfortunately, the ideology that has instead gained most momentum is one that encourages us to lash out at our neighbours and blame them for the lack of prosperity and worth we feel in society. Sadly, as has often been the case throughout history when looking for the cause of a structural problem (or at least something to blame), many have opted for the classic (though lazy and spurious) target: the immigrant. We have begun to act with a sort of all-encompassing protectionism; we have retreated behind our borders and built higher walls. This has paved the way for some shocking events.

"Everyone's preaching to their choirs, Words billow up and get trapped in church spires"

I wrote this album during twin shit-storms: the election of Donald Trump, and the run-up to Brexit. The pervading social zeitgeist at the time was one of increasing division. The general polarisation of political opinion was the frustrated reaction of vast swathes of society who felt left behind. Social media was enabling a ramping up of this vile atmosphere, with its unique ability to incubate echo chambers and confirmation bias. We only 'follow' the people we agree with; we interact with those who hold the same political beliefs as us; in advertising and in the news, we are shown again and again, 'if you like this, then you'll like this'. Algorithms give us more of what they know we like. We are steered away from encountering anything outside of our comfort zone.

Using the imagery of a church spire felt apt as, historically, religion has been the most prevalent force in dividing humanity.

"We're fed up with all the cyanide"
We have become increasingly cautious, suspicious and distrustful of other views
as we become part of separated networks, completely disjunct from one another
as groupthink takes over. When we do encounter a belief that does not chime
with us, we react with immediate anger because we are unpractised at reasonable
discussion and our views, now so reinforced, feel like part of us. An attack on our
beliefs registers as an attack on our very being. Almost all political discourse then
becomes embittered, uncharitable and spiteful.

"Sparking fury against one's neighbour, Twisting the truth with a blamethrower"
Of course, sensationalism in the press hasn't helped, fanning the flames of tribalism,
polluting calm and rational debate, and twisting truth to suit political agendas.

This polarisation encourages us into a position of fundamental conservatism. By
that, I mean we remain in our small areas of comfort and distrust everything
outside of them. New views are not considered, and progress therefore cannot come
into fruition. Society becomes static.

The obtuse phrase 'take your country back' is just one example of a train of thought
that is persuasive to a worrying number of people, mainly because it's simple to
understand and doesn't take into account any broader analysis of society's core
problems. It is far easier to get someone to be emotionally stirred when talking
about the invasion of 'your' land by 'other' people than it is to say, 'our problems
are complex and mainly result from inbuilt systematic inequalities relating to
capitalism and modern democracy'. Pinning your frustrations on another human
(especially one who looks different to you or who has a background in another
culture) is easy and quick to satisfy.

This completely ignores the fact that immigration brings ingenuity,
entrepreneurship and diversity, as well as being a net positive on the economy. It
completely ignores the fact that inequality (not immigration) is the basic driver of
almost any negative social measure, from life expectancy to mental illness, violence
and literacy. It completely ignores the fact that it is the banking and finance
sectors and our evangelical devotion to the free market economy that has vastly
increased inequality. It completely ignores the fact that climate change will be
displacing colossal numbers of people all around the world, as formerly populated
areas become uninhabitable ("feel the rising tide"). It completely ignores the fact

that 'national identity' is an abstract and evolving concept; countries and cultures expand and shrink, emerge and die, and borders and walls only further divide humanity at a time when all the problems we face are global in their effect. It completely ignores the fact that 'divide and rule' is the oldest trick in the political handbook. The powerful and privileged use media outlets to inundate us with frightening propaganda about the worst aspects of other cultures in order for us to stay blinkered and overlook the crimes of the financial class ("That burning rage could gut a castle, But you torch your neighbour"). And finally, it completely ignores the fact that distrust and hatred towards others unmistakably creates a distrustful and hateful social fabric ("and now your whole town is ablaze"). We have seen this in the rise of hate crimes and antisocial behaviour as communities become more divided and public safety becomes further threatened.

Angelic Studios, Brackley, UK. 2017 – Tom Pullen

AIRFIELD

A Field

Desolate
And underfoot
A tarmac river flows

I wait to depart;
An inconceivable art
When you're no wings and all elbows

Oh, it's so cold
I watch my breath unfold
It wraps us in a cloud of gloom

Through adversity
Hope must not
Become the casualty

It's common for people to believe
Everything happens for a reason
I'm sorry that's false, and it's poison

But even if there is no purpose
To the things that you have gone through
An ordeal can reveal an airfield

Stop, disown fear
And I'll be here
If you need a friend, my dear

So, you're down on your luck, you're down
Yeh you're down on your luck, you're down
But that don't mean you're out
No it don't mean you're out, now

When the wind's against you, remember this insight:
That's the optimal condition, for birds to take flight
Now the wind's against you, don't give up the fight

Due to an almost counterintuitive law of aerodynamics, it is much safer and easier for planes to take off whilst flying into a headwind. At London's Heathrow airport the wind usually blows from west to east; therefore planes fly to the west on take-off as they use less energy to become airborne. Similarly, large birds opt to take off into the wind as they expend less energy doing so. This felt like the perfect metaphor for staying determined and motivated during a period of adversity. The wind, this mighty element, may be against you but it can also lift you to greater heights.

Hardship can often result in some form of positive outcome, be it personal growth, learning something about oneself, becoming stronger in some way, or simply becoming more experienced in dealing with that particular hardship, diminishing the shock and paralysis when confronted with a similar experience. It makes one better prepared. I describe an aeroplane's take off as an 'inconceivable art', not only because it still baffles me when watching the sheer size and weight of these mechanical beasts becoming airborne, but because during a period of hardship it is often inconceivable to think how this will one day be thought of as something that helped you. When caught up in a difficulty it is hard to see a bigger picture.

The airfield I had in mind when writing this was nothing like the controlled chaos of Heathrow Airport. I envisioned instead the long-abandoned RAF airfield I'd visited on a family holiday as a kid: the grass growing through the cracks in the long unused runway or 'tarmac river'; the faded markings and the old ruins of the storage buildings. A setting of a decrepit, desolate and 'cold' airfield felt apt as all too often we face our hardships alone.

One thing I always try to avoid with my lyrics is positivity for its own sake: relentless optimism. I never want the lyrics to fall into the pot of being platitudinous. I want to be realistic when approaching difficult subjects and experiences, so I wanted to make sure people didn't misrepresent the essence of this track as being akin to the laughable platitude 'everything happens for a reason'. This is my most hated of all sayings, as it manages to be both terribly ignorant and arrogant at the same time. There is no 'reason' for going through hardships. There may well be a positive outcome (as I am stating in this track) but that doesn't mean one was 'meant' to go through it or that there was purpose or justification for the hardship itself. To say so would mean whoever or whatever 'designs' these 'happenings' and 'reasons' is one cruel, sadistic bastard.

Hardships can, of course, trigger some unforeseen silver lining, but sometimes that is not the case. We can only hope that through every trying experience we will at least emerge a little wiser, perhaps simply more equipped for life's ups and downs. This piece is heavily influenced by Shakespearean perseverance; his work is littered with great statements on adversity and moving on such as, 'Let me embrace thee, sour adversity, for wise men say it is the wisest course'[1], 'The robbed that smiles, steals something from the thief'[2], but most of all, 'Sweet are the uses of adversity.'[3]

1 *Henry VI*, Part 3: Act III, Scene 1
2 *Othello*, Act I, Scene 3
3 *As You Like It*, Act II, Scene 1

RABBLE ROUSER

I torture rockstars with pliers
They're so stock
It wouldn't be a shock if I opened them up to see wires

I destroy all amplifiers
People climbing over bodies like spiders
I'm onstage with a face like a sack of screwdrivers

It's gonna be a showstop, roadblock
And we are the epicentre, the bedrock of a new sound
I say "we're coming for you"
And I say it with a face like a sack of screw screw screw screw

What's your criteria?
Complete hysteria
Decibels so maxed you can yell out your deep secrets
Nobody's gonna hear ya

What's your medium?
Complete delirium
The lunatics took over the asylum...
On guard

Warning, this escalates quickly
Are you getting nervous?
The mist rolls in thickly
Are you getting nervous?
Have you lost your nerve?

What's your technique?
So so so so unique
Fuck ego, minimise the self, maximise the bond; the clique

What's your business here?
Sit back and witness sheer chaos
You can't keep track of the hell we raise…
On guard

Sweden, Dec 2018 – Tom Pullen

'In Celebration Of The Spark'. North American Tour, 2018 – Andrew Rousell

The lyrics to this track are basically a description of *Enter Shikari*'s live performance and the atmosphere at our shows. Effectively, this is my job description. There isn't much more to say on the subject; I believe it to be wholly self-explanatory to anyone who has been to an Enter Shikari show.

Lyrically, it is in the same world as 'Warm Smiles Do Not Make You Welcome Here', a song about the big difference between art as a form of human connection and art within capitalism, which is often simply thought of as a form of commerce. The 'torture rockstars' line is me being critical of the banality and narcissism of many modern 'artists' who – usually down to a lack of imagination or talent – rely on ego and rockstar antics to sell their music, rather than any particularly interesting artistic content. I try again to separate what Shikari do with hyper-capitalistic music, by relaying what a live Enter Shikari show has always and will always be about, focusing on the connection, the communion, the loss of self and ego, the unity of all present.

REPORT ▮▮▮▮▮▮▮▮▮▮	CASE # 07
SUBJECT OPERATION: THE SPARK	OFFICE USE ONLY LEAVE EMPTY

FROM THE DESK OF: AGENT REYNO
FAO: ▮▮▮▮▮▮▮▮▮

we are the dust

    on the stained glass windows

trying to comprehend

    the cathedral

'Shinrin-Yoku. Classified internal document' by Richard Littler, text by Rou Reynolds

SHINRIN-YOKU

Surrounded

Sunk deep in the dense embrace of the forest
I imagine this is the polar opposite of suffocation
My lungs seem to gain extra capacity here
And I feel like an empty inbox
As I contemplate the ultimate assault course
The roots, the stumps, the branches

I squint into eternity
As I try to get to grips with the fact that
We have no idea what we're dealing with

My lungs fill with air
I feel supercharged, now

I'm hyper-aware
I shiver and short circuit at the depth of the universe

We are the dust on the stained-glass windows
Trying to comprehend the cathedral

Just as art is often simply thought of as a commodity in a free market economy, so is nature. This inspired me to write what can be thought of as an ode to nature. A celebration of our landscapes and ecosystems and the source of beauty and replenishment they can be for us. We're lucky enough to have recorded our music in some amazing studios around the world, almost always located in secluded rural areas surrounded by beautiful scenery, rich in wildlife. This is perfect for me, as a walk in nature often helps calm my mind and properly focus my attention for writing music or lyrics. This is reminiscent of how I would write in my head walking home from school. These were the days before smartphones with voice recording apps, so everything I created would have to be committed to memory. I would often take the longer, more scenic, route home, dawdling whilst repeating melodies and rhythms that had popped into my head until I was confident they were memorised, alleviating my fear of forgetting what I was convinced at age 11 would be my first hit single! So it was no surprise to learn just how beneficial spending time in nature is to our headspace and health in general.

This track is inspired by two Japanese concepts I have recently become fascinated with, *Shinrin-yoku* and *Yugen*. Both are majestic concepts and are difficult to translate simply and directly into English. *Shinrin-yoku* is best translated as 'forest bathing', a term coined in the 1980's to encourage Japanese citizens towards healthier lifestyles and preventative healthcare. Put simply, it means taking calming walks through forests. We all know intuitively that spending time in nature is good for our wellbeing, but there are now countless studies to corroborate the calming and restorative effects of a stroll through the woods. The reduction of stress is one just one such example, and one I reference with the line, "My lungs seem to gain extra capacity here and I feel like an empty inbox".

Yugen is a harder concept to translate. Though it is not a religious term, it is used to describe things that are real and tangible, yet so profound and powerful that they cannot be successfully contemplated or fully described with words. These could be fleeting moments of clarity when everything seems to make sense, or fleeting moments of disorientation when everything appears too overwhelming. It is often during these moments of tranquillity, during nature walks when we are free from distraction, that our minds begin to ponder the broad and the abstract. I label this as being 'hyper-aware' (and being an INFP[1] I'm prone to daydreams of this kind regularly). For years, a recurring experience of *Yugen* would arise whilst thinking about the sheer expanse of the universe; I would feel intense stupefaction but also an almost magical feeling of insignificance, however paradoxical that may sound.

"We are the dust on the stained-glass windows, Trying to comprehend the cathedral."

---

1 Introversion, Intuition, Feeling, Perception (Myers-Briggs Type Indicator)

Southbank, London, UK. Summer 2017 – Jennifer McCord

243

'In Celebration Of The Spark'. North American Tour, 2018 – Ian Johnsen

Osaka, Japan. April 2018 – Tom Pullen

UNDERCOVER AGENTS

And I said "park your car and come on up to my house
We'll plan a revolution"

And I said "yeh, I think I'm ready to begin
We'll destroy the disillusion"

I am currently under construction
Thank you for your patience

We veneer and veil, we present a cold disguise
We're all undercover agents

It's only in our heads
I'm so done with the pressure
Yeh we try to control everyone's perception
I'm done with the weather
Trapped in the mist I can't find myself

It's only in our heads
I'm so done with the pressure

And I said "if you want to go far and wide now
We've got to go together"

Tonight I'm howling with the wolves
Yeh I'm howling, can you hear us now?
I was seeking another life
And the moon was so bright…

It's only in our heads
I'm so done with the pressure
They twist and control everyone's perception
I'm done with the weather
Trapped in the mist I can't see the truth

It's only in our heads
I'm so done with the pressure

Park your car and come on up to my house
I want to see your body
I don't want the gloss, I want to see the truth
I want to see your body

My inspiration for this piece came from one of the most pervasive struggles in modern life: that of 'perception management' – a rather dry term to describe our ability to influence or control how other people perceive us or, indeed on a broader scale, how people perceive events and ideas. We are all perpetrators and victims of it.

At its most extreme, it is the diligent sculpting of our interpretations, or the twisting of truth. I felt compelled to focus specifically on two of its forms that we all witness on a daily basis, both of which can be devastating.

First, in our personal lives, our evolutionary requirement to be accepted (or to be part of an 'in-group') urges us to present a carefully regulated form of ourselves. We go to exhausting lengths to guard or hide certain aspects of ourselves, and at no point has this become more achievable than now with the advent of social media. Technology has bestowed upon us greater power than ever before to shape how people see us. We can restrict information or edit and filter reality to our own liking – "We veneer and veil, we present a cold disguise".

It's almost cruelly ironic that this behaviour, which fundamentally stems from anxiety (specifically, the fear of being ostracised), becomes a source of even more anxiety. When mindlessly scrolling through Instagram feeds, we're inundated with the rose-tinted highlights of people's lives (as we all filter the content we put out into the world); a relentless 'best of', which almost always leads us to perceive our own lives as inferior or somehow lacking. It's understandable to want to share our success and happiness with our social circles, but we didn't foresee the negative effects of this when it's on such a large scale, propelling the rise of depression and anxiety in modern society.

Of course, this isn't an entirely new problem...

"I'm so done with the pressure"
Since Edward Bernays[1] told us that sex sells, the airbrushing and photoshopping of models and celebrities to create an unrealistic and unvaried perception of the human form has been a great cause of anxiety and self-loathing for many people, women especially. In the age of social media, we have all begun to take part in this reality roulette; this circus of perception. We experience a compulsion to join in, indulging in a visual 'keeping up with the Joneses' through fear of being thought uncool, ugly or somehow inadequate.

"I'm so done with the weather/Trapped in the mist I can't find myself"
The weather is something omnipresent, impossible to escape, I use it here as a metaphor for perception controlling behaviour as it feels so reinforced and critical throughout society at the moment. And in being so pervasive it can easily lead us to lose a sense of who we really are as we are caught up in the pressures it creates.

"I don't want the gloss, I want to see the truth/I want to see your body"
If openness is a central theme to the album, then the last verse is my call to everyone: don't gloss over your true self. We are all human beings, far weirder and more grotesque, queer and idiosyncratic than we give ourselves credit for. Honesty is very rarely the wrong policy.

The second form of perception management that influenced this piece is the attempt to control public or group perception; it's the framing of the news to benefit or advance a political agenda, or the broader fight for control of the narrative.

"They twist and control everyone's perception/Trapped in the mist I can't see the truth"
Campaigns of misinformation, biased reporting, and exaggerated stories are as old as news itself. Every journalist knows that sensationalism has sold more newspapers than straight fact has over the years. But, again, with the invention of social media we've seen things come up a gear. In the most extreme cases we have seen completely fabricated stories. The now infamous article, "Pope Francis shocks world, endorses Donald Trump for President", was posted during the lead up to the American presidential election by a Macedonian cottage industry who were collecting the ad revenue from platforms like Facebook as their many false articles went viral. This highlights the monetary incentive to inventing false claims, as well as obvious political incentives.

"I am currently under construction/Thank you for your patience"
With an album predicated on honesty and openness, perception management felt like an important social criticism to address. I did want to make it clear, though, that I was not writing this piece from some lofty detached position, but from the ground, fidgeting anxiously in the 'mist' myself. I too have hidden things about myself; I have lied about myself and I have fallen for fake news; I have commented and reposted things without checking their authenticity.

"If you want to go far and wide now, we've got to go together"
Each one of us is afloat in a sea of peculiar and potentially damaging social phenomena, and we must all address and conquer them.

1 Edward Bernays (1891-1995), an Austrian-American, and also Sigmund Freud's nephew, known as 'the father of public relations'.

Gin & tonic image from The Spark CD booklet. Photo by Agata Wolanska.
Photo editing/layout by Richard Littler

The Spark. Limited edition cassette design by Richard Littler

Brixton Academy, London, UK. 2019 – Tom Pullen

THE REVOLT OF THE ATOMS

I woke in a fluster
I saw my walls disintegrate
Before my very eyes
Now that was a surprise

I looked out my window
I saw houses fracture and dissolve
Straight into thin air
That gave me a scare

It's the revolt of the atoms
From London Town to ancient Athens
Eliminate all traces of human life
They plan to wipe us out

I found some intel
The atoms had conveyed, convened and connived
To the sound of my alarm clock
Now that was a shock

Helium spoke first
It cooled tempers and lifted spirits
But then it made a threat
And that made me sweat

"When truth gets left untouched
It accumulates like dust"

Everything is crumbling

I wanted us to have one anomaly track on this record – something surreal and absurdist. I missed writing tracks like 'Mothership', which is essentially a piece of science fiction. 'The Revolt Of The Atoms' details the experience of one human being who wakes up to a world where all atoms have become sentient overnight. The atoms have conspired to destroy every trace of humanity after concluding our species to be parasitic and threatening (yes, I *was* reading a lot of Franz Kafka at the time of writing *The Spark*…).

The story begins *in medias res*, as we are thrown into a surreal and distressing plot ("I woke in a fluster, I saw my walls disintegrate"). This is a direct nod to Kafka's classic books *Metamorphosis* and *The Trial*, in which he throws the reader straight into the action with no introduction. I adore the disorientating nature of this style. Having my protagonist wake up to immense distress is a further nod to Kafka's protagonists, Gregor Samsa and Josef K, who wake into a panic-stricken and surreal situation.

The line "when truth gets left untouched, it accumulates like dust" is a piece of communication from the atoms themselves, conveying their reasoning for our extinction. I wanted them to communicate in this pompously poetic, almost faux-cryptic way, like they were killing us off with a knowing and contemptuous grin. With this line they are saying that when one refuses to notice or accept truths, those truths will become unavoidable and cast a shadow over everything. So the literal dismantling of human matter is our comeuppance for our self-serving behaviour in devastating ecosystems and destroying the opportunity for sustainable life on this planet. With the endless repetition of the line "everything is crumbling", I hope to create a trance induced by the realisation of the severity of our own current situation. Even if the walls aren't literally crumbling around us, we're certainly on the right path.

Birmingham, UK. November 2017 – Tom Pullen

AN ODE TO LOST JIGSAW PIECES

I awoke with a face like a crumpled plastic bag in a puddle
When everyone in this town has a bag for life, he said
My life is a total mess
It's 8pm and I'm not even dressed
And oh how I miss your prosecco glazed lips
I miss them like the majority of modern mainstream music misses an original
metaphor for missing someone

I was so scared of confronting the world alone
Fear put me in a headlock and dragged me back from the unknown, so…

If this is a siege, I'll wait this out
But I'm full of doubt

I tried to defend our castle walls
But the attack came from within the halls

They say that time heals, so I'll wait this out
But I'm full of doubt

I'll wait this out…

I may backtrack on these words one day
I may orphan what I'm about to say
But in my chest there's a thundering pain
It feels like God's in there, having a migraine

And this is tough, man
I've lost more pieces of my jigsaw
It don't seem worth making now, Nan

They say you've got to stay busy
I'll keep my mind occupied on the here and now
Cos you're not with me
But that's ok, we'll cope somehow

We all cope somehow

The French essayist Michel De Montaigne once said, "Many, many things that I would not care to tell any individual man I tell to the public and for full knowledge of my most secret thoughts, I refer my most loyal friends to a bookseller's store." Books have always been a comforting refuge for the inquisitive, the struggling and the lonely, not only for the reader but for the author too. Subjects can be explored calmly and slowly in solitude and then presented before the world for consideration.

Creating and listening to popular music also serves the same helpful function. With this piece I gave myself time and isolation in order to explore carefully two recent experiences of loss.

"I awoke with a face like a crumpled plastic bag in a puddle/When everyone in this town has a bag for life"
The first movement of the piece concentrates on the feelings of disorientation and desperation I felt when coming out of a long-term relationship. For anyone north of 30, when almost everybody around you is 'settling down' and having children, this can be an especially jarring and lonely ordeal.

"I was so scared of confronting the world alone/Fear put me in a headlock and dragged me back from the unknown"
When you've spent a sizeable proportion of your life with another human being, your sense of self merges with that other person. Your two separate egos almost feel like they combine, so a breakup can often feel like losing a limb, or worse, an actual attack on your perception of 'self'. So the process of discovering that you can, in fact, live without that other person and you are, in fact, still a whole entity, can be a very long and arduous one.

I fought against this for a long time thinking I was nobly fighting for the relationship but, in fact, I was selfishly and illogically fighting for the reassuring comfort of normality.

Moving on requires you to redirect your feelings of belief, confidence and hope, from believing you can singlehandedly save a failing relationship, to the possibility that you can survive without it. Redirecting your hope from the known (and therefore comforting) entity of the relationship, into the unknown (and therefore frightening) zone of independence is a difficult task.

The second movement of 'An Ode to Lost Jigsaw Pieces' is about the loss (in the literal sense) of grandparents; something I'm sure you've all been through or will go through at some point, dear reader. It was first birthed as a standalone instrumental piece for strings which I wrote after the death of my Nan. After a year or so I endeavoured to add vocals to the piece but unfortunately (and with the added emotional weight of nostalgia) it was too affecting, and every attempt I made to record vocals ultimately failed as my singing quickly turned to something closer to snivelling, spluttering or whimpering.

The lyrics are mainly inspired by the powerful empathic pain one feels upon witnessing a loved one try to keep it together after the death of someone close to them. For me, it was seeing the pain my parents and brother felt after the death of my grandparents. In this movement I am addressing friends and family, often specifically, by adding the colloquial 'man', and then 'Nan' with the line "I've lost more pieces of my jigsaw/It don't seem worth making now, Nan".

I wanted these lyrics to be a window into the conversations that happen in times of hardship. As a side note, I immediately knew when I started writing the lyrics for this song that a jigsaw puzzle would be the perfect metaphor, as my Mum, brother and I would often sit down to make them with my Nan back when we lived together as I was growing up.

The piece ultimately ends on a raw but quietly hopeful note, "we all cope somehow", highlighting the importance of family and friendship in helping each other through these times of loss.

These are essentially examples of the partial removal of my life's support framework. The absence of stability and consistency makes us feel unsafe and vulnerable and all we can do is be frank, patient and kind.

Osaka, Japan, 2018 – Tom Pullen

STOP THE CLOCKS

Stop the clocks
I'm killing time
I don't ever want this to end
And you said "That makes two of us"

There's a cinema in me
It plays counterfeit scenes
All my worries and blunders
And you said "That makes two of us"

Where's this present you speak of?
Where's this heavenly bliss?
I'm so sick of time travel
And you said "That makes two of us"

And all your life you just exist
And all your life it's moments missed
And all the time you wait in line
What d'you find?

Drifting, my life is unmoored now
Give me coordinates please
I look for a safe harbour
And you said "That makes two of us"

This piece is a celebratory ode to human connection. I set out by describing the inner turmoil related to the worrisome mind, to rumination (the "cinema" is that big screen in our heads that plays an endless loop of fears and worries), but I then repeatedly fixate on how elating and even alleviating it is to discuss these inner experiences with others. Sometimes just hearing the phrase "that makes two of us" from someone (or words of a similarly reassuring nature) can help us realise that we aren't faulty, we aren't an anomaly and we aren't alone.

My journey with mental health only really began once I started opening up about my inner experience. Anxiety (with its constitution of negative assumptions and biases, and peculiar influence on one's sensations and behaviour) is a typical human experience and not an idiosyncrasy. Finding this out enabled me to be aware of what fuels it, understand its influence, and most importantly begin to combat it.

"And all your life you just exist…"

I'm frustrated that it took so long for me to open up about my inner experience. From secondary school onwards, I wish I'd had the education in mental health and the opportunities to flag personal difficulties. Though educational structure and societal ignorance must take a proportion of the blame, my shyness was the main thing I personally blamed for a long time, though of course that itself can be an influence of social anxiety! I found that the fear of embarrassment or ridicule stopped me from communicating my inner experience but this in turn furthered my mental anguish, as my diffident nature became something I detested for making me miss so many opportunities (e.g. introducing myself to people I wanted to talk to). The whole bridge section (ending with the sardonic question "What d'you find?") illuminates my annoyance with the influence anxiety has had on my behaviour. (I must add a parenthesis here that I've since learnt just how easy it is to slip into self-contempt when evaluating and criticising one's own behaviour, so one thing I'm practising going forward is self-acceptance and self-love).

"Where's this present you speak of?"

This verse is all about meditation and trying to live in the moment. We regularly live our lives on autopilot, not fully aware of what we're thinking about, we're held hostage to our wandering minds and their imagination. Mindfulness meditation is all about spotting when that state is taking over and causing us trouble. Being able to choose whether we want to continue down whatever rabbit hole our hyperactive mind has led us down can give us a greater sense of space, control and focus. Comparing this ability to "time travel" felt apt for two reasons, firstly because we must literally wrench our attention away from ruminating over the past or worrying about the future and bring it back to the present, and secondly because time travel is supposedly impossible, which can certainly seem to be the case with regard to efforts to be mindful!

"Drifting, my life is unmoored now, give me coordinates please"

One of the classic – if not the classic – worries is "what we should be doing with our lives?" and most people when pushed for an honest answer will admit they don't really have a plan or know with any degree of certainty what they should be doing. Learning this can also be of some consolation. I think the ubiquitous question "what do you want to be when you grow up?" – as if there's only one thing to be and you should have a solid idea of that almost from infancy – is an extremely damaging one. Schooling can be uninspiring, work can be stultifying, relationships can be complicated and exhausting. I doubt anyone on this planet has their life completely 'sorted', and if they tell you they do, it is more likely they are distracted, ignorant or simply self-unaware.

Learning this is another step to realising we're all just bumbling our way through life, trying the best we can with varying degrees of luck and support. Connecting with others (especially over life's hardships) is one important thing that makes it all so much more bearable.

Leeds, UK. February 2019 – Corrine Cumming

INDEX OF FIRST LINES

22nd of June, 209AD 99

A field, desolate and underfoot a tarmac river flows 230

A heedless and harrowing future is developing 62

A naked eye conspires with fear 181

And I know that we've still got time, but I do not think we're invincible 72

And I long for you to appear 40

And I said "park your car and come on up to my house, we'll plan a revolution" 246

And I'm thinking what's the deal with the facts they conceal? 81

And what comes next? 55

And with these humble tools we can trigger any emotion we choose 135

Analysis of the human race in 2011AD 111

Are you staying awake for the lift off, tonight? 214

As one child is taught red on his mother's knee 163

Axiomatic subject matter, executed with absolute lucidity 103

Bury it, that's not what you want 33

Can you hear the war cry? 172

Come and join the party leave anxieties behind 118

Deck chairs out lads, here's the spot 47

Doctor, fetch the anaesthetist, I want to go under the knife 167

Drip drip drop, bit by bit, it's the dulcet sound of the glacial melt 178

Each nation used to provide its country with security 98

'Ello Tyrannosaurus, meet Tyrannicide 141

Get me the manager! 199

Go tell all your friends that this is the end 17

Here behind those eyes there is something you should know 140

Here tonight I clock a thousand heads 65

His eyes are locked on her 21

Huddled in this acid nation with apprehension 48

I am a mindsweeper, focus on me, I will read your mind 196

I am upper class, upper middle lower class 189

I awoke with a face like a crumpled plastic bag in a puddle 258

I don't want to take my country back, I want to take my country forward 224

I know that we're gonna repeat history unless we sort this out 122

I lie here staring up at the stratosphere and hoping we're gonna get out of here 86

I never walked on the moon 192

I refuse to notice the wind or the rain 185

I torture rockstars with pliers 234

I wanna live outside, live outside of all of this 220
I woke in a fluster, I saw my walls disintegrate 254
I'm biting the blade of your scissors 53
I'm gonna paste you up, cover you in wallpaper 77
It's your future and this is gonna change everything 115
I've been hiding here for a thousand years, waiting for your ghost 13
If our own lives aren't directly affected then it don't need to be corrected 70
If there's one reason to smile, it's when you look up out at night 201
Let this battle commence, one last time! 42
Like Socrates I only graze on the slopes 175
Mate, I'm zonked absolutely spent 79
My heart beats in my head and it's thunderous 151
Now I don't know about you, but 130
Now I was feeling like a total giant! 88
Now let's cause some fucking havoc 87
Packing the last few shirts into a bloated suitcase 142
Previous wars made millionaires out of billionaires 126
Rise, taste the air, lock and load 37
Scratch card glory or waist low pleasure? 34
Shikari was a third generation Aztec 101
Simmer down ladies and gentlemen, you're acting rather irresponsibly right now 90
Stop the clocks I'm killing time 263
Sunk deep in the dense embrace of the forest 239
That's the sound of another door shutting in the face of progress 123
The air turns black, the birds drop from the sky 23
The Lions are at the door, we ain't taking orders from snakes no more 80
There was a house in a field on the side of a cliff 112
This is an appeal to the struggling and striving stakeholders of this planet 158
This is the voice of God, you got it? 206
To be strung up on a leafless tree where everything dies and nothing grows 148
To take away our expression is to impoverish our existence 153
To the multi-storey car park with our friends 94
Today for the very first time we started planning out the ultimate crime 109
We're trapped in the ribcage of a wilderbeest 45
Where's your respect? 25
You might never meet me, for I am King 30

Angelic Studios, Brackley, UK. 2017 – Tom Pullen

INDEX OF SONGS

Acid Nation 48

Adieu 40

Airfield 230

All Eyes On The Saint 99

An Ode To Lost Jigsaw Pieces 258

Anaesthetist 167

Antwerpen 88

Anything Can Happen In The Next
Half Hour 21

Appeal & The Mindsweep I, The 158

Appeal & The Mindsweep II, The 196

Arguing With Thermometers 123

Bank Of England, The 185

Common Dreads 62

Constellations 142

Dear Future Historians 192

Destabilise 109

Enter Shikari 13

Fanfare For The Conscious Man 98

Feast, The 45

Gandhi Mate, Gandhi 130

Gap In The Fence 86

Havoc A 80

Havoc B 87

Hectic 94

Hello Tyrannosaurus, Meet
Tyrannicide 141

Hoodwinker 206

Jester, The 90

Johnny Sniper 37

Juggernauts 72

Keep It On Ice 53

Kicking Back On The Surface
Of Your Cheek 47

Labyrinth 23

Last Garrison, The 172

Live Outside 220

...Meltdown 115

Mothership 17

Myopia 178

Never Let Go Of The Microscope 175

No Sleep Tonight 81

No Sssweat 25

Ok, Time For Plan B 42

One True Colour, The 163

Pack Of Thieves 140

Paddington Frisk, The 148

Quelle Surprise 111

Rabble Rouser 234

Radiate 153

Rat Race 151

Redshift 201

Return To Energiser 33

Revolt Of The Atoms, The 254

Search Party 122

Shinrin-Yoku 239

Sights, The 214

Slipshod 199

Solidarity 65

Sorry, You're Not A Winner 34

Sssnakepit 118

Stalemate 126

Step Up 70

Stop The Clocks 263

System... 112

Take My Country Back 224

There's A Price On Your Head 189

Thumper 103

Today Won't Go Down In History 30

Torn Apart 181

Tribalism 101

Undercover Agents 246

Wall 77

Warm Smiles Do Not Make You
Welcome Here 135

We Can Breathe In Space,
They Just Don't Want Us To Escape 55

Zzzonked 79